DATE DUE			

NEW VOICES
IN
AMERICAN POETRY
1973

New Voices In

COMPILED BY

VANTAGE PRESS

American Poetry

1973

THE EDITORS OF
VANTAGE PRESS

NEW YORK   WASHINGTON   HOLLYWOOD

FIRST EDITION

Published by Vantage Press, Inc.
516 West 34th Street, New York, New York 10001

Manufactured in the United States of America

Standard Book No. 533-01162-0

New Voices In American Poetry
Compiled by the Editors
of Vantage Press

CONTENTS

INTRODUCTION

NEW VOICES IN AMERICAN POETRY—1973 is the second volume in a series of annual anthologies compiled by the editors of Vantage Press.

The enthusiastic reception which greeted the publication of the 1972 edition of NEW VOICES confirmed our belief that there is a need in contemporary literature for such a series.

NEW VOICES IN AMERICAN POETRY—1973 continues the tradition of providing poets a medium of their own through which they can place their work before the public and the critics.

The Editors

my poem 282-253

NEW VOICES
IN
AMERICAN POETRY
1973

This Anthology is given
to the Rutisill Library
By —
Edy the Beam Mayes
Member of the Rutisill —
Beam Clan
of
Lincoln County

A SONNET TO THE SIRENS

Of yore on Capri's magic sunsoak'd shore
The Sirens' song lured seamen on the seas.
To heed meant Death, though men were promised ease
From sorrow, toil and strife forevermore.
Those bird-claw'd women revell'd in the gore
Of any guileless victim they might seize.
Capri's blue sky above and sultry breeze
Enhanced the mystery of their treach'rous lore.

The Sirens now a diff'rent song disclose,
When giant war-birds black the heavens' blue
And with a deadly aim their deadly eggs dispose.
Their song saves landmen now, though weird and shrill,
From Death more baneful than the ancient Sirens knew,
And grants brief respite t'enjoy Life's sweetness still.

* * *

GREEN RIVER, UTAH

The land you channel is still your own,
Though men have come and men have gone!
For your silt, which builds for a day and a day,
And your banks, which your gnawing has cut away,
Are made and destroyed, as a child at play
Both molds and shatters his blobs of clay!
Great Green River!

You have seen the savage pushed back and back
By the ceaseless press of a wagon track!
Then along came the steel rails laid in pain,
And the beetle-buzz of a wide-winged plane.
But you know, as they came, they will pass again,
That nothing matters save God's sun and rain!
Great Green River!

1

THE PONDERER

The answers come slowly as thru a fog,
  Dim headlights slowly approaching,
Clouded by the swirling mists of comprehension
  That only increase my fear and tension.

What should really be very clear to me
  And without any reservation, answers to equations,
Are at the moment roadblocks to my mind.
  As the the answers I try to find.

What has been once learned should be forever kept
  In some secret mental file in the head,
And examined at my leisure and my pleasure.
  Only in this way can others try to measure

What I should have already learned in time past.
  Things necessary to my very existence
Should become clear to me, and be expressed at last,
  That I might say with confidence: I know. . .

But time and tide wait for no man, these are facts
  Like the brackish tidewaters of the sea.
Many, many unused facts repose in me;
  To expose them requires some positive acts.

Reading, reading, and read some more;
  Add more facts to your mental store,
For only facts have any value or worth
  That new ideas might thereby be given birth.

So my fellow studiers, know that you are not alone.
  At times I think my mind is made of stone,
And what should be my thinking machine
  Is only the figment of a dream.

Wesley M. Alden

MOON ROCKS! MOON ROCKS!

Moon rocks! Moon rocks!
   The rarest things upon this earth.
Because they are scarcer than diamonds,
   Who knows what they are worth?

They may be igneous, aqueous, or sedimentary,
   Or bits of lunar lava anciently spilled.
They may be cosmic dust and heavenly slime.
   But from a landscape never tilled.

Brought back from the reaches of outer space.
   By venturesome sons of earthly man.
One little peek into the cosmic plan
   That allows us to live as sons of the human race?

The cost to us in dollars has been billions,
   All of small value, the stars are numbered in trillions.
Some clowns would play us tricks
   And display bits of common bricks.

Display the trickery for all to see
   Just to test some trusting fellow's gullibility.
The trick was good—it hit its mark;
   The trusting fellow had his say.
After all, they were just rocks, any way,
   Not diamonds or rubies or emeralds,
Or even a piece of cosmic slime or glass. . .
   Just rocks from another sphere,
About the same as you would find here.

REASON AND PURPOSE

"Why don't you quit?" a loved one asked me, smug;
"Why do you waste your time and strife this way?
You spend these lonely hours all alone
For nought! You never will get rich this foolish way!"
Can they not understand my need to write?
To form in spoken word the yearning deep
And unrealized in every living soul?
When in the dark of night a dream begins
To leap—and tumbling, stumbling phrases, one on one,
Come pouring forth till verses write themselves.
I read the finished lines and marvel whence
They came. I only know my dreams are here inscribed.
And so I keep on writing down my thoughts.
So what—if never a poem my comfort buys?
Must men be paid for drops of falling rain?
Or woman for her child's small trusting eyes?

* * *

A NOTE OF SYMPATHY

I penned a simple note of sympathy.
Communion of my lonely heart with yours.
You did not feel the need of quick reply—
You knew that I would know—and understand.
When next we meet, a handclasp,
Soft and brief; and tear-dimmed eyes
Will prove our friendship deep.

TRUTH

Stilled for a heartbeat on the greening breast;
This boy-man, with the half-born spring attuned,
Hearing alike the ancient call to recreation,
The living, breathing reason, just to be.
With instincts sharp, they wait the age-old sign,
The essence of the universe, endlessly renewed.
Then, at a predestined sign unheard by Man,
In unison, God's directing hand is verified.

* * *

GRANDMA

Watching my children's children;
This all-absorbing pastime of parents of parents.
In each small face I see a trace
Of my dead partner, these many long years gone.
There—just there—a wisp of smile,
A glint of mischief; he was master champion
Of perpetrating mischief!
In each small voice I hear a song
Of generations, joined, in these—my loved descendants.
I pray the prayer of motherhood,
Once, or twice, or thrice removed, but poignant;
Bless these tiny souls unto Thyself;
Preserve to their inheritance our dreams.

Gail Rudd Angel

TOUCH ME. . .

Touch me. . .
And let it be not a question—
Not a sly seeking nor a blind demand,
But a clear, straightforward answer.
The city's weeks have left me bent.
I weak and weep and curve
To shoulders on the subway,
Elevators full of warmth.

Touch me. . .
Come between me and the wind—
Not a wall of woolen shoulder just between,
But come around me snug and thick.
The ice has tautened me into a wire.
I shake and shadow from
The astigmatic eyes,
The generalities of smiles.

Come over, over, over me
And settle all around me like a heavy quilt.
The worry-work has left me childish in my fear;
If you are not going to touch me, don't come near.

WHERE ARE YOU GOING?

Where are you going,
and how can I change
within your hand?
I'm only smoke
You cannot hold me. . .
Stay

Are you standing still?
Then I am moving back
and forth
before your silent eyes
I cannot hold you. . .
Go

LE MAXIE

Amorphous clay is yet defined—
In callous rock, dimensions new—
Patient hands with secret goal—
Seek within the compassionate soul—

Infinite grace in infinite meaning—
The silent depths emerge in form—
By degree in elusive flight—
The darkness, yet, reflects the light—

Ominous heights, infrequently scanned—
A fleeting moment in greater quest—
Transcending love and transforming hate—
Shaping the course that channels fate—

This poem is a special tribute to Le Maxie Glover, sculptor.

* * *

NOTHING

From that which passed—still passing—finding another,
Yet, lingering in dissonant vibrations of elusive truths—
Oversimplifications of undersimplifying utterances
Of simplicity—We speak!

And knowning nothing—pondering all—Declare!
Having been and seen—We feel!

But, that which turns tickled fools toward nostalgic heights,
And tempts a corpse to fancy life;
Oh, noble reprieve, spin thy infinite tapestry
And leave compassion in thy wake.

Touch!—That flies might course the designs of her spidery web
And bid her welcome—come breakfast—

8

LADY SOUL

And Miles saw her when he sketched across Spain;
Wes took her to the seventh planet and they had
        lunch at Quincy's Universe;
Blind Ray met her in Georgia and she gave him the blues;
She moved to Harlem years ago.
From New Orleans, I think.
They used to call her "Lady Day"
        in the 40's
Then it was *Dinah* in the late 50's
started calling her "Nina" after that;
some folks still do.
Nancy and Dionne say she changed her name to "Aretha"
a couple years ago;
She used to hang out on Beale Street when she was runnin'
around with "W.C."
When she come to Harlem she had quite a thing goin' with
a cat named "Bird" over on Fifty-Second Street;
Later on tho' she got tired of him and starting tippin'
around with a dude named "Dizzy",—some chick, eh?
That ain't the half of it, man
she left him for a Monk.
I guess she finally got into a religious thing
Last time I saw her was at the Met, or was it in the village
No man, wait
It was over to "Funky Lou's Place"
Yeh man, that's some place. You oughta check it out.
You don't know where it is?
It's right down the street from "Funky Isaac's Place"
where else, baby—where else—

9

IN THE LIGHT OF THE MOON

To sit out in the cool of the evening
And smell the peaches on the trees,
And the fragrance from the apricots drying on the trays—
These were all at Grandpa's house in the old days.

What precious memories when upon Grandma's knee
They said, "The first one to see the moon come over
    Bear Mountain, holler."
No one but Grandpa and Grandma would bother
To hear a baby yell, "Whee-ee-ee-ee!"
When that heavenly disc over the mountain glowed.

A little later in life a walk down the lane in the evening. . .
What love was expressed to show the Big Dipper and so-and-so
Up there in the Heavens in the moon's glow. . .
But when they talked about the Man in the Moon
That made a little mind wonder;
With a bundle of fagots on his back
How a child wishes she could see all that!

Or to hear Grandpa wonder and ponder
About planting time;
It's time to plant this, for it's the light of the moon.
Next month will be the first quarter;
Before that, we'll plant in the dark of the moon what we
oughter. Can't that moon stay out
And not go away
When Grandpa has to plant for his hay?
Then Grandma would say,
"We'll trim her hair tomorrow while the moon's full you know,
Because that's the right time to make it grow."

Quite a little later, the braids and the legs got longer.
With Grandpa it was a glorious thrill
To walk in the moonlight, still.
Holding the lantern for him to see to shovel the gopher holes,
Instead of flooding the field of uncut hay.
In the quiet, cool, moon's light,
Still trying to see the Man in the Moon.
When the glow was so calm and soft and clear bright
I knew he was out that night.
I tried to see the fagots and his face
But trusted Grandpa knew what was right,
And felt the love and heavenly peace in the moonlight.

Those walks in the moonlight
Gave a heavenly feeling of peace and tranquility.
That big round moon, so beautiful and serene,
Made this spot below a place of enchantment,
Greater than any earthly scene.
Big, round, beautiful moon,
Sending that light and silvery glow
On all the earth below.
How wonderful to look up and see
You, and feel the rest and tranquility
When it's evening and still in the light of the moon.
Those things a child can feel and know,
Who loved to walk down the lane or on the ditch bank
With Grandpa and Grandma long ago,
In the moon's pure light and heavenly glow.
They can never take that moonlight love
From me——because I know it's from above.
They may bring back a rock or stone
But from here the Man in the Moon is still on his throne.

Louise B. Armstrong

CREATION EVERYWHERE

There is no place where God is not;
Under the sea and in every spot
His manifestations are there to behold;
Whether on the burning desert or the mountain top, so cold.
Every place has its tree or shrub or grass or flower,
A bear, a giraffe, a lion, cougar, camel or tortoise—
They are all there, each in its own place,
Fulfilling the reason for being and the great Purpose.
Put them all together, man's habitation is a Heavenly bower.

There's darkness and light, sunshine and rain;
Together they complete each year
Fulfilling the cycle. It's all very plain that
Where Life is, God is.
Life is everywhere we are,
So God is everywhere, near and far.

There is no place where God is not
From the deepest ocean to the mountain top.
His manifestations of renewing Life and Beauty in every
        place holds true,
From the depths of the sea, the hills and valleys, and
        in the sky so blue.

For man, His promise is real.
The Bible says, "If I make my bed in Hell, Behold, Thou
        art there."
Where is there anyone who cannot feel
In looking back, and know
His uplifting Power protected him,
Even when in sin?

But for that promise of mercy and grace
Everyone could be in a far worse place.
If in us alone, our paths and destinies thrived
It would not be so sweet to be alive.

Space and time are one with Him,
That Eternal Power will never dim.
And God holds His Creation with Love and Mercy and Grace—
A Universe which time and space can never erase.

* * *

UNFOLDING PETALS OF A ROSE

Deep within a rose, every facet of life has been
Drinking, breathing, growing, even making a new seed,
Working and sleeping, divinely guided—
It's all done from within.

So much more has man in store
Every facet of perpetuating life is from within
And takes place regardless of his lack or sin. . .
How much more we could show
If we trusted more!

Like the roses, unfolding, expressing, possessing,
        reflecting Beauty, all from within;
As the bud reaches forth to the sun, a petal opens;
Deep colors catch the light and fold back to bring in
        and reflect more. . .
It's opening chalice shows a soul
That trusted and says,

"Look, see what beauty was closed up in me!"

Why can't we trust more?
And live to know what Nature has in store?

Louise B. Armstrong

Beauty in the rose—
Beauty man can show—
He has unlimited Power to grow
All growth is from within.

Is there as much of God in the tiny flowerette
As in the mighty earth, water, and sun from whence it came?

If so, what of man, whose origin is in the Image and Likeness
    of the Creator of all?
Does he reflect the Spirit of all of these?
Can he say, "Look! See!
What Infinite Beauty and Love
Is vested in me!"

BEAVER

We had five sons; we named one Beaver,
He grew up fast smart and eager.

He was sent to the war in Vietnam for worse or
better,
But only God knows in heaven how I felt when I
received that letter.
The only thing I could see, Beaver was gone forever.

Beaver, Beaver, why did you go away and stay, never
to pass on earth this way?
The days are long and the nights seem dim, but
I hope we meet again some day.
Although you are out of sight, we think of you
day and night. . .

I don't know where and I don't know when, but with
you in our hearts, I hope we will meet at our eternal
end.

GONE IS THE BABE WITH HAIR OF GOLD

Gone is the babe with hair of gold,
Gone is the little boy whose hand I'd hold,
A young man stood there in his place
Pure of spirit, fair of face. . .
I will speak my thoughts aloud
Of my dear son I was so proud.

James is my dear son's name
Friends always called him *Jim*
At their cruel and senseless whim
They sent him to a battlefield afar.
I did not wish my dear son to go;
Alas, he did not know
Nor understand
This was to be his death command.

Gone is the babe with hair of gold,
Gone is the little boy whose hand I'd hold,
Gone is the soldier brave and bold;
This sadness is too often told.

EXPECTATION

Expectantly, go forth from day to day
   Alert to revelation on the way;
A word, a look, a handclasp sent from God
Can stir one's soul and lift it from the sod
   To heights where Saints and Angels dwell.

   Go forth! There is no uneventful day,
Nor uninspired, though duty in much drabness lay.
   As bursts a shaft of light on shapeless clay,
So radiates God's love and grace our way,
   Illuminating shadows gray, assuring one
Of brighter spheres than this.
   Pilgrim, take heart and wonder, work and pray!

FROM WHENCE WE CAME

To lift himself up from the earth
Prompted man to dream;
To venture further from his birth
Required one grand scheme.

He was suddenly a child again
Dressed in odd disguise,
Wandering through a fairyland
Wondrous to his eyes.

Earth below! A blue Capital O—
Suspended grandeur.
Instantly gone are feelings of woe
Replaced by adventure's lure.

An awesome view—like fantasy;
Prisms in delicate lace,
Star jasmine, violets, anemone
In deep seas of outer space.

Hark, the meteor's sprinkling gold
Through perpetual twilight,
Behold the man, as seemingly bold
In majestic wingless flight

Man's visions then did manifest,
Filling him with pride,
For space beyond became his quest.
God granted one giant stride.

Perhaps it is from whence we came
A long, long time ago,
Dreaming dreams the very same
As He who made it so!

THE POSTER

Psychedelic poster plastered to the ceiling.
Well-worn mattress plopped upon the floor;
Eyes staring from their host
Thereon flopped.

Orange room reeling.

Cold plank frames a smaller indentation
Wine-stained stuffing
Pours weeping from the gores;
Red wads matching tear for tear.

Lamentations. Lamentations.

Perched off balance atop the table
As unsteady as himself,
He clutched the poster proper,
Then placed it, crushed,

Adjacent. "Her" epitaph.

Amidst evaporating trickles
Scattered capsules turned maroon,
Reefer butts disintegrating
In empties strewn about the room.

All matching emptiness with emptiness.

LOVE

I am beautiful; you have made me
beautiful. Your warm body
flowing love, lying next to mine.
A tender touch,
penetrating—
like drinking too much wine.
Although
there is no light,
(my eyes are closed)
I see your gentle face, your smile.
Rapture, delight,
enfolded in your embrace,
conscious only of you; my disembodiment.
While
the unimportant
part of me dozed,
the real me seemed to float above.
Your mouth on mine,
unwavering,
no need to search;
savoring
the well-known
softness of our love.

SELF-DISCOVERY

Once, when I was half-past ten,
I strolled alone through Rolling Glen.
'Twas there I spied two turtle doves
Engrossed in feathered love.

With guilty thoughts it should be quelled
A strangeness from within me welled;
Silk-sweatered warmth in one grand surge.
I had a sudden urge

To cuddle nude in tall, cool grass,
Delighting in its soft caress. . .

A cherished memory of when
I was half-past ten.

AN ANGEL CAME MY WAY
(To a friend, who is very kind)

My heart was full of grief.
I thought for awhile
God had forgotten me;
I couldn't even smile.
Then I stopped to think—
What evil have I done?
When I said my prayers
My worries were all gone!
Then someone came my way,
Wearing a big smile

On that sunny day,
His eyes were shining bright.
As I spoke to him
I felt my Lord had touched me,
I experienced a whim
Then my grief was released.
He brought me peace of mind
Which I greatly enjoyed,
'Cause he was so kind
And always full of joy!

THE SEASON OF THE SEAS

Was a story,
The Season of the Seas;
Told in silence to me
Thru words of hollow winds.

Was a poem,
The Season of the Seas;
Told in scenes to me
Thru eyes of running tears.
            Filled with hope;
            Filled with heart;
            Filled with anguish
            And the time to depart.
Deserted seas.

* * *

PROTECTION

The satin quality of the sun
Is the fabric of the day—
But it is not felt *this* day.

The wool quality of the clouds
Is the cover over the sky—
Protection.

Eva Beaver

ANALYZING OUR EMOTIONS

In trying to analyze our emotions
Too often we feed the spirit of unrest;
By virtue of quality is destiny governed
And mastered techniques of living our best.

We learn by experience before we believe;
Taste ecstatic bliss and trembling doubt
Before we fully analyze the difference
And know the need of what we do without.

Strength is measured when we are tried
In the fires of life, its exacting scroll,
And character is formed by various emotions
Felt in the heart of the human soul.

Nothing is by chance, there are reasons;
Not one tear or sorrow is in vain,
We profit by the ever-increasing knowledge
That life continues to give us in pain.

We must have sorrow to know what is joy;
See the weak to know the strong;
Associate happiness with doing of right,
And sorrow with that which is wrong.

And out of the chaos of our emotions,
When we come to analyze them close,
We find the most simple things in life
Are the ones that satisfy the most.

Princess Orelia Benskina

HOPE

Nurtured are my dreams by the hope for which I live each day:
The hope to laugh, love, live, and my dues to my God, pay.
Hope, which through my being. . .serenely and silently, surge
In the search for peace, health, and happiness in abundance
to splurge.

Hope that will rekindle the heart that has lost its spark
In the impetuous desire to sing again like the lark.
Laughter which brings joy to a pair of saddened eyes,
Perpetuated through the dreams of love which hope compromise.

Hope can start the heart in motion. . .
Be it a kiss, a touch, a smile, or a thoughtful notion.
Whichever, it doesn't matter, for the heart's a tune
To the frequency of love's voltage, from which the heart is
not immune.

Hope is a prayer or a kindly word; even a pat upon one's back;
How consoling is this to someone whose heart is lack—
Often trodden, ensnared, and depressed; whilst trying
desparately to cope
With those who may deceive, or their motives digress. Yet,
where there's life. . .there's hope.

JE T'AIME BEAUCOUP

Though I'm shy and perhaps a little frightened, too;
My heart to you, cries out: *JE T'AIME BEAUCOUP!*
It's not a love that's transient, inane or snide. . .
It's just amicable, tranquil and even timorous of being
cast aside.

Filled with the yearning for your sanctuary. . .this
supplication I offer each day:
For solace and impunity, which only this lonely heart's
confession can convey.
From time to time I often sit and retract my thoughts. . .
only to find
Your smiling face there, searching every corner of my mind.

Not being able to resist you, here in its nakedness my soul
stands;
Imbued with this dauntless rapture. . .that which your heart
commands.
Henceforth, until this body is freed from my soul. . .and I
pray, not you;
I will continue to cry out: *JE T'AIME BEAUCOUP!*

THE GRADUATE

A little boy I once knew
Had a hard time as he grew;
Childish colds, sick and pale,
And always with an anguished wail.

But his mother's loving care
Gave him life and love to share,
And through tears I heard her say
"He'll grow to be a man one day."

I watched him grow from year to year
Baseball, football. . .what a fear!
Lose or win, I'd see him grin
And Ma was there to comfort him.

And yesterday he won a "charm"
A school diploma beneath his arm,
I saw him smile at Mother near
As if to say, "For you, Mother dear."

* * *

MENDING

I've mended broken dishes
And often a broken toy;

I've mended torn-up pictures
And found it lots of joy.

I've mended many articles
With tiny bits of string,

But I cannot mend my broken heart
For I've tried most everything.

Constance Marie Benson

TO SHARE WITH YOU

I'd like to have some pretty clothes,
Some jewels and hats and shoes,
I'd like to have a lovely car
To drive where'er I choose.

I'd like to have a nice new home
All furnished bright and gay,
With roses growing all around
And trees that nod and sway.

I'd like to live and love and laugh
With babes to smile and coo,
I'd like to know this happiness
Was shared, sweetheart, with you.

* * *

MY ONLY SIN

I always try to be so good
For life just seems as if we should,
Especially at the countryside
Where peace and quietness abide.

The mountain roads with flowers tall
The beautiful summer, spring and fall;
The sparrow and its mate chirp high
While robin redbreast flutters by.

All goodness seems within my soul
But there's a truth I must unfold;
It's just a little hurt within—
My love for you is my only sin.

MY LITTLE MAN

I washed his little face and hands
And combed his baby hair,
I gave him all the tenderness
A loving aunt could share.

I took him to the circus
When he was only three,
Never heard such merriment,
Such happiness and glee.

I taught him how to ride a bike
To roller-skate and swim,
There wasn't any type of game
I wouldn't master just for him.

Through high school and through college
I crammed and worried, too,
I came out knowing nearly
As much as Nephew knew.

Today he wed and I did cry
"For shame," came friend's retort;
They could not see the picture
That was passing through my heart.

IN THE BEGINNING. . .

In the beginning, a heart full of love,
Sweet, overflowing, the goodness He shared;
Then was created an image so pure
Beauty forever was meant to endure.

One day thereafter, a heart so saddened,
Children unworthy, the anger He loosed;
Then came disaster, a darkness for all
Just the intention is left to recall.

Thru the centuries, a heart of pardon,
Sacred covenant, a reprieve He gave;
Then a sacrifice, the merit to save
Perfect atonement to release each slave.

In the finale, a heart of justice,
Master of wisdom, a verdict He'll give;
Then comes rejoicing, if Heaven it be
All eternity, the mystery to see!

* * *

THE MASK OF GOD

The sands of my desert are hot with pride,
Burning each footstep as I wander on.
Quicker I go, but the pain eases not,
Running and running, each downstep so heavy,
Unable to bear the suffering for long;
Only a halt lets numbness set in.
Peace floods my soul, the waters I seek;
Then stillness and quiet break open my heart—
"Let it burn! Let it hurt!" the Sun seems to say,
"Stay in the desert tho you know not why.
My light comes to guide, the blessing you asked,
Thru dryness and wounds, My waters are masked."

H. Lee Benson

UNWORTHY THO I AM

To awake from quiescence enkindled with love,
The dawn of perception, with hope to respond. . .
Such daybreak so joyful, laud billows the heart
Unworthy tho I am, another new start.

To relish the privilege of empyreal warmth,
The noon of enticement, with trust to pursue. . .
Such midday so peerless, a gift to treasure
Unworthy tho I am, my worth no measure.

To accede the splendor of celestial plan,
The eve of fulfillment, with faith to accept
Such vespers so tranquil, in wonder to rest
Unworthy tho I am, this life is blest.

* * *

ON AND ON. . .

Roaming and searching, wandering thru life,
Stumbling with each step, with nothing in sight,
The sands of life's desert seem never to end.
Parched and dry, my soul cannot speak;
Barren and empty, I thirst for Your waters.
The mirages are many and lure me on;
Reaching out for relief, I stumble again.
Strength slowly ebbs, tho still I push on.
On thru the endless sands of myself.
Tho I swagger and sway, one more step I take,
Another and another, blindly pushing on—
When, my God, will You take all strength?
When will I know no more steps to take?
When will I know to just lay down and die?

RONDEAU

You fool, to be so stubborn blind!
Your fingers could a pattern find
To weave in threads of purest gold.
To all, your heart is overbold
In letting Bacchus rule your mind.

You weave this hour a web designed
For foolish men. To youth you hold
The chalice high, as time grows old,
      You fool!

Talent given to mankind is
A torch to hold aloft, to wind
Around the span of life. You have sold
To Bacchus and his world your mold
Of betterment: your mold, mind,
      You fool!

* * *

THE SPICE TREE

Sun shines high on the spice tree; gazing
Upward we cannot see the spice spilled
At our feet, until in odd moments its
Spiceness we meet. . .Youth cannot wait
To wear the hoods of writer's great. . .
Wishing wings fly high, not knowing gazing
At the sun blinds one. . .when in chimney
Corner years feeling stirs within hearing,
Artists play or sing; hidden chords come alive
As on a cello string. We realize with tears
What might have been through the years, we who
Were once young. . .but life is almost done.

TO ALICE GRACE

Star flowers afield
are discontent
        to yield
to storm and wind;
beauty to give
        they must,
so upward they grow
knowing
        stardust.

Flowers unfold beauty
as they reach their height;
so do minds
        filled
with knowledge and light.

* * *

THE MARY KIND

Queens have loving hands,
Cupping faces, they understand
With heart and mind
        very much the Mary kind. . .

Amid opened lily buds,
Mine rainbowed, sits beneath the Throne
telling haloed cherubs
        of earth's beauty she has known. . .

THE HIRING BOSS

The hiring boss
Walks his pier,
Knowing every step of the way,
Full knowing every step it takes
To get his job,
Every step it takes to hold it.

As he walks
He hears the restless whispers
Just beyond his ears,
Calling out words beyond endearment
That make the job what it is:
The domination of the strong man
Over the weak
That the weak may live,
That the work may be done
For families to be fed,
For food to be put on the table.

Nobody likes a boss,
Even less a hiring boss,
And the boss knows it
As he walks his pier 365 days a year,
To laugh, smile, wave,
Return their hushed endearments
With a look,
His look,
The look of the one in charge
That mocks their derision,
Tells them he knows.

It's fine with him
As long as they keep on working,
Unload the ship,
Earn their pay
That their families may eat,
That the hiring boss, like all the rest,
Can go home, be human again,
Love, feed his own family.

* * *

LIFE-LIGHT

Your love
Lights the darkness of my soul,
Enabling me to see beyond the nights,
The hopelessness of my blight
Reflected
In the sounds and the sights,
The smell
Of my dirty tenement hallways.

Your loving smile
Is my life-light,
Lighting my thousands
Of tenement days and nights,
Filling me with hope
Where there was never any before. . .
Before I met you.

BABE

Never. . .never
Leave me, Babe,
For without your love
I would surely die.

I love you, Babe.
I love you with all the love
The human heart can hold,
To love you more today
Than I did the day before.

Babe,
You're all sunshine and laughter;
Just by walking in the door
You fill me,
Illuminate all the dark corners of my heart,
Making me unaware of sorrow
Ever having dwelt there.

You're special people,
Babe,
Having a gift
Only a rare few possess:
To use a word,
A smile, a gesture,
To make people feel their worth,
Feel they're important
For what they say and do.

I can't be sad with you, Babe,
For you're the icing on the cake,
All the hope of better tomorrows,
All hellos
With never a goodbye.

THE DON

The gunmen,
His soldiers,
Were alert
To their Don
As they lined the stairwells and hallways
For him to pass by in safety
To his mother,
Who lay dying in the back
Second-floor apartment.

Weary,
Tearful-eyed,
All of sixty-five years of age,
He humbly climbed the stairs
To pay his final act of respect
To the only person he ever loved
In a lifetime.

The police
Knew he was coming
And stayed away,
Knowing
Many would have died
That day
If the Don had been taken,
If the Don could not pay his last respects
To his mother,
To give her a son's—
The Don's—last kiss goodbye.

EACH DAY I DIE

Each day
I die,
Sick to my soul,
Nevermore
To know
The nearness of you.

You never
Told me
Of your illness,
Or of a time
When I would never see you again.

One day I awoke,
Turning to kiss you
As I always do,
To find my kiss grow cold
Upon your cheek,
To find you gone.

Neither
All the human understanding
In the world,
Nor all the warm, tender comfort
Of well-meaning friends
Can reconcile my heart
To accept your loss.

For by your loss
I lose a part of myself
Each and every day,
To know
Each day I die.

VERY DEEPLY FELT

Knowing there is one who does care,
Each night I say a little prayer
And I *know* that He will hear
A prayer ever so sincere.

Hoping that each day will be
One of health that makes you happy;
Less aggravation, more relaxation, too
Praying for the best to come true.

* * *

ODE TO A DIRECTOR OF NURSING

A smiling face and tender heart
Is the only way I can start
Saying something about a person like you,
Even though *much* more is true.

May He whom we often think of,
Bestow many blessings from above;
Happiness now, and may the future bring
You the Very Best of Everything!

LIFE'S ONE MOST VALUABLE LESSON

Newborn babe, here is the best wisdom you may learn;
Prayer is the balm supreme who for Him do yearn.
Whose paths to seek and follow, ideas to share?
Youthful sapling in time of need, who will most care?

When moon recedes to chambers before rising sun,
To silent beds dimming stars do fade, duty done,
Heavenly hosts praise One, Unison, really best;
Each day starts anew, young child, chance your faith to test.

No parental opulence can character build;
Vain riches blow away like chaff when grain is milled.
Sheer wealth will not shield you always from falls or wrongs;
Wisdom to tell the future to no man belongs.

The only true foundation your roots to strengthen,
Is nurtured in courage your sweet days to lengthen.
Heed! Live not in abandon, no true direction;
Lasting values have only one right selection!

Then youth, now parent, with newborn to bear your name,
With quivering lips, trembling hands, and shaking frame;
Which? Sad tears of sorrow, or joys of thanks will reign?
Learned your life's lessons yet? Prayed with deep inner vein?

Now, not young, mid life's bridge; Aging? No longer bold?
Your spirit torments? Time to search; how honest, soul!
Listen, heaven's flames flash, piercing your fearing mind!
Do white shapes in the blue write your life harsh or kind?

In the quiet of yourself survey and reflect,
What good you could have done but forgot in neglect.
Of what worthiness are you actually proud?
None? There must be some! Shamed to proclaim them aloud?

Morris A. Bloom

Mountains climbed, rivers swum; earthly boasts, worldly fun?
Ego! My, what a hero, for such contests won!
But have you fed poor mouths? Dried tears? Eased someone's
pain?
These the true medals, gold letters, which write real fame!

Now naked in your thoughts, earnest, or yet at play?
Ah, once child! Made your journey poor? When lost the way?
Now is the time! Your Father may yet save the day;
Seek Him with faith, piety—learned how to pray?

Your last chapters are written in the Book of Deeds.
Obsessed with self-reproach? Still time to plant good seeds.
Allay your worry, frail one. Be at ease, pause, rest;
Believe your heart. What comes in peace, the very best!

Life's paths were before you when a child, one to choose;
No crystal balls, lures enticing, potent for fools;
Precious lessons from the Mount, faithful, enduring;
Start now! Learn knowledge from those lines, reassuring.

The very last moment when life's light dims, not clear;
If mindful presence is lost, and you feel Him near,
His warmth around you happily begins to flow;
A well-earned repose will on your tired visage show.

Blessed those who, well-learned, for others do care;
Of themselves they give, thus more they receive to share.
Prayers sincere? Of all evil your soul now shorn?
Forward into a realm unknown! Be again born!

TOWER OF DIGNITY

I

Let me never lose the human touch;
Let me feel as mine the mordant crutch,
The prison of the paralytic's bed.
Mine be the blood by hero or by traitor shed,
The laborer's yearning at day's end for rest;
Each baby's head be nestled on my breast.

Mine be the feet that trudge through endless dust,
Following a coffin, down paths of rust—
Blind, through fathoms of undeciphered time;
The composer's dialogue with the sublime;
The plowman's poem to the churning earth;
The mother's torment in the vortex of birth;
The soul's last cry in death's dark undertow;
The poet's knowledge of the ebb and flow
Of universal rhythm; the cyclorama
Of the ever-changing human drama
Of which I am a part and a beholder—
That which is ever-new and ever-older.

Mine be the hands that heal, unswervingly kind;
And mine the solitude of the demented mind;
The prisoner's compound, the monastic cell;
The factory whistle, the cathedral bell;
The corrosive, filth-infested tenement;
The jungle village—steaming, pestilent.
To share the deep serenity of age,
With one who's written well his lifetime's page;
The laughter of a child, who is free to run
In sudden joy through wind and molten sun;
The alcoholic's tenebrous temptation;
The mystic's vision and peace in meditation.

The ecstasy of love, the doom of pain,
Compassion—like a life-endowing rain;
The sweeping arc of human panoply,
From lullaby to final threnody,
From psalmist's glorious paean to beggar's whine:
Let these be mine, O Lord—let these be mine!

II

Mine be the homelessness of the refugee,
The terror of those oppressed by tyranny.
The orphans' desolate, bewildered tears
Be in my eyes; their quiet sobs engulf my ears.

The color of the segregated race
Be mine. I take upon myself the face
Of the Untouchable, the erstwhile slave,
The peon, the coolie. Mine be that common grave
The martyred Nameless were forced to excavate
For their own tomb. My voice must join the great
And ever-swelling chorus of men who cry
Out for a chance at true equality, defy
Those who sustain the ghettos and the caste
Delineations of the outworn past,
And call to men of every race and creed:
"Let Humanity at last be freed!"

Mine be the hands that pray—then build a tower
Of dignity for each, beyond the power
Of prejudice and narrow cults and hate—
That men may seek their God-appointed Fate!

CONTACTO

(After seeing Toby Joysmith's
Bas-relief painting: "Contacto")

I

The tumultuous earth is open, harrowed, plowed.
Man sifts the land and claws with long lean fingers
The soil beneath the evanescent cloud.
A pygmy and a half-grown giant, he lingers,
Muses, yearns for the invisible crest.
His feet caress the warm and pungent clods:
The ochres and the sepias of the breast
He knows. . . And yet, he lifts his gaze toward gods
He cannot see or touch—whose presence beats
About him like a thousand cloistering wings.
The mounting vision slowly melts the sleets,
And liberates a cardinal that sings
And cleaves the heavens with its sudden flight:
A man born blind receives his partial sight.

II

Then from his sienna earth he sculptures clay,
And from his umber soil he tries to give
A form to formless vision: to build a causeway
Between the tangible known and the fugitive,
Intuitive surmised. And from the rocks
He builds a pyramid. Its massive base
Is earth-rooted, but its sloping blocks
Scale newer heights in search of timeless grace—
Its vertex pointing toward the Infinite.
And all infinitude awaits the hour—
Poised above the planet to transmit
What magnitudes of light and stellar power;
And man toils upward in his slow ascent,
His spirit stretching toward the firmament.

III

And from the wood of forests he fashions chapels
And pagodas, climbing silent latitudes,
While inwardly he struggles, strives, grapples
With gravitational pulls. . . Infinity eludes
Him, though It spirals toward his central core.
And so, from stone of quarry and of field,
He builds a thousand towering temples for
The unknown deity his faith would shield.
The spires of cathedrals lift their hands
In prayer. And sometimes there are shafts of light
Upon the altars of anointed lands—
And man attains incalculable height.
And plunging downward through celestial galaxies
God holds his soul in luminous vortices.

IV

And man, through gradual self-elevation,
At determined points in space and time,
Is caught up in the fire or revelation
And ascends the blazing spiral of the sublime. . .
And the Godhead—within the measureless scope
Of Its compassion, traversing universes
To fulfill man's millenarian hope—
Establishes a channel, and immerses
Him in blinding plenitude of light.
And he becomes the bearer of the Word,
Participating in the cosmic might
Through the sonship he has been conferred.
Across a chasm only the Spirit could span—
The Creator accomplishes His union with man.

CUP OF LIFE

The Master pours the cup of life
We must accept and drink.
It is a mixture quite unique
If we but stop and think;
The dizzy heights of bright success,
The depths of dark despair,
The bitterness of sorrow
And the sweets of joy are there.
So if your cup seems bitter
And no hope you have found,
Perhaps you haven't stirred enough
To spread the sweetness 'round.

* * *

WHATEVER

Whatever the cares or joys of the day,
The world rolls on its appointed way.
Whatever the heartache,
Whatever the hope,
The housewife must linger
With water and soap.
And whatever portals
Swing open for me,
Must wait 'til I've bandaged
Poor Danny's skinned knee.

BE PRAISED, MOTHER

Be praised, Mother,
To have been born from you,
In my youth to be loved from you,
Be praised, Mother.

                    Be praised, Mother,
                    To have guided me on Sunday
                    At the praying assembly,
                    Be praised, Mother.

Be praised, Mother,
To have made me understand
When I was an adolescent,
Be praised, Mother.

                    Be praised, Mother,
                    To have understood together
                    That I wanted to be a traveller,
                    Be praised, Mother.

Be praised, Mother,
To have given me the last word
In letting me go around the world,
Be praised, Mother.

                    Be praised, Mother,
                    To have waited for me
                    And to pass away before me,
                    Be praised, Mother.

Be praised, Mother,
You up there in Heaven,
Truly you are my confidant,
Be praised, Mother.

THE SONATA

Night. . .
Thoughts come to the pedestal of the black lines of
        beginning and end. . .
A complete train of dreams is waiting
In the space before the station to which all the roads lead.
The signal is down,
Recognition is meaningless;
There is no stationmaster.
The signalman is drunk in the saloon;
Patience is running out.
On the standard the red signal shuts off passage
And the signals are not moving at all.
Before the power to comprehend all inspiration has stopped
Only waiting has passage.
The lowered signal guards the shores of lovers,
The weeping echo of the river that has flown by is coming
back.

The morning is asleep on the cheeks and lips of a girl,
And the greed of dark is swallowing up her golden hair.

The sonata is waiting for a melancholy dawn. . .

A young man is coming with a glass empty of hope,
And he lies in the mud with his head on the track.
Trains are grating in both directions at the beginning
        and the end

With their cold wheels. . .

On the platform a redcap is walking and greeting aimlessness.

REASSURANCE

Down on earth, life flows a shining rivulet,
Its many splendors the melodies of a minuet.
Light, brisk and heavy steps on sidewalks,
Crowd noises mingling with love-talks;
Drugstore counters hum with mild chatter,
Homebound held to witness raindrops patter.
Multi-colored autos moving swift and slow,
Traffic signals flashing red, green and yellow.
The mailbox as usual painted red and blue,
A symbol of contact, to lost treasures a clue.

Up in heaven, fleeting snowballs roll around
In the vast blue ethereal playground.
Leaves rustle in crisp afternoon air
Caressed by the wind's poignant care.
And I behind some stone wall laze and dream
This vision of uninterrupted lifestream.

My precious moments are changed in solitary towers
Into a solid mass of mechanical hours,
But the portraits of life my dreams contribute
Are to the lifestream the greatest tribute.
I step out and reach for the sublime pleasure
Abounding in life in a bountiful measure.

THE SENTINEL

A lone signpost stands
          On a desolate piece of land,
Marked by footprints of years
          On the sprawling sand;
A solitary watchman named Conscience
          Keeps the vigil endless;
The signpost is his symbol,
          And the land, a mind in duress.

Mary F. Boss

MY PRAYER

A million thanks, dear Lord, for entering
                into my mind and heart.
You have given me the gift of knowledge and
                the grace to use it wisely.
Thank you, dear Lord, for making Life
                a little lighter,
Because, as time goes on, you have even
                made it brighter.

* * *

TO MOM, WITH LOVE

If words of love could bring you near,
I would wait and wait
Until I'd hear
Your enchanted voice unfold
Sweet words of love without a tear.

I love you more and more, dear Mom,
With each passing day;
Your smiling face and silver hair,
Those hazel eyes that shone so clear,
And the cheeks that always seemed so fair.

And when the days add up to years,
I'll always save all my love
Just for you, Mom, dear.
And I'll still write
With all my might:
"To Mom—With All My Love."

A LULLABY

A lullaby with me the birds do sing
To put your soul at rest;
A pretty song with a childish ring,
Words easy to digest.
It says in three words
What could be said in four.
They are the words "I love you,"
Only these, none more.

* * *

PAIN

Pain precedes happiness,
Bliss of the human soul.
Joy comes only thereafter,
Or so we are told.

LOVE'S FIRST EPITAPH

Here lies my love, highly disdained
        and covered with sorrow.
A hapless love, so pitiless it
        never saw tomorrow.

* * *

SPHERE OF LIFE

Life is but a confined sphere,
Open there and enclosed here.
In this sphere there's joy and pain,
A lover's kingdom—my domain.

* * *

THE ESSENCE OF LOVE

They tell me I'm in love
With you. . .and I listen.
They tell me I'm a fool
To love. . .and I smile.
I tell them life is empty
Without love. . .and that
Makes it all worthwhile. . .

EPOCH OF LIFE

I have released myself from worry,
I have left my soul to play.
I have ended my hurry-scurry,
I'm at the epoch of my life today.
I have surveyed the golden moon,
I have seen the rising sun.
Tomorrow will never come too soon,
'Cause my life is done.

* * *

A BEAUTIFUL MAIDEN

She smiled such a beautiful smile—
Unselfish, ingenuous, and infantile.
She spoke with a softness unheard,
A euphonic chatter, the chirp of a bird.
Her eyes gleamed like a million suns,
A wayward star, a comet that runs.
Her body was more beautiful than a budding rose,
The fairest of all maidens, the one I chose.
In hyperbolic splendor my love I extol,
A beautiful maiden who won my heart and my soul.

ODE TO LOVE

I have loved a rose
 and pressed her face up to my brow so lithe I'd faint
 and drown within a pool of tears from out her eyes—
 two orbs like pleading waifs.
A rose with petals braced straight into the airy spume,
 her body fragilely curved into my heart,
 a useless ragged piece of mortal matter.
For what beauty, looking wide upon her face,
 that time with her lovely lips must sure have traced.

I have loved a rose,
 not many are the few
 with crimson red damask of pastel hue;
A rose—her cheeks a fading moon,
 I have with tender press enraptured soon.
A rose—she has no voice,
 but speaks of unborn silence;
 she speaks to me alone, she tomes of auras, unborn child,
 and how forever floats with a phial,
 a phial filled with dreams of her own immeasurable self
 and forever tilting her heart with her white breath.

I have loved a rose,
 her presence rains a warm flowery shade;
A rose who has within my darkness layed;
 the hurts within my ragged heart were stilled,
 when the little rose put forth her hand and filled
 the sadness in my heart with violets and pansies cheering.
Oh, smile that was performed upon her lips,
 such burning that set the hopeless agony in me yearning.

I have loved a rose,
    and felt upon her bosom the dark that could its night
    turn into sun's most glorious rising;
A rose with nose exquisite turned upon a leaf careened
    in joy's cool lather;
    a rose a little beauty drop dancing forth into a pond,
    landscaped blue green fairies' wand;
Simple essence, my little rose,
    great to highest thrones behove,
    naive prancing carefree be,
    my little rose so happily.

I have loved a rose,
    and my heart would bleed till my soul pined,
    if her rose would bloom no more in my soul shined.
Ah, rose, her rose I have loved from heaven's mouth,
    climbed forth to chant my song of her so faint,
    her rose would wither from the blast,
    such words that stream forth from the unmade dream
    to encompass my precious rose in soul's high honor.
To the sweetest being where precious chattels
    like roses dawned and budded,
    are watered with the blood of love that died,
    and has embraced all beauty in its veins in a cosmic
    starry flow.

FALL OF YEAR

The thinning leaves expose the bare beneath the trees;
The shifting, wilting branches swing lazily with ease;
The lucent leaves are paling golden, green, and pink.
Their fallen browning sisters lie drying on the brink
Of wind-tossed lost farewell, in trembling flight distressed.
The dark trees hiding, biding, still in their divest—
Solemn, naked, sullen—shy in their last dress.
Remnant pale and tattered—leaving less to guess;
Dripping, dying leaves, each baring blacker twigs;
Thinning, fading, baring raw fingerlings in rigs;
Shedding their last vestige of glory—lush, full-blown—
To stark and darkened harshness, prepared for colds unknown,
And only memory lasts, golden as a chime,
As leaves remembered, falling, sadly, from time to time.

TUCK ME AWAY

Tuck me away
        in a corner of your heart,
Tied up
        in a little pink ribbon of Love,
Tenderly, tenderly,
        forget me.

* * *

AFTERMATH

The cigarette is crushed,
        and its last wisp of smoke
Fades in the room that's hushed
        of talk and mirthless joke.

The cigarette is smoked,
        and its ashes smoulder gray
In a tray with friends invoked,
        who have burned and gone their way.

Anne Sophia Bullard

A DREAM JUST FOR YOU

In depth a child, later on a woman grown,
And in you a seed is sown!
For a Poet surely you will be,
Your eyes can see the things that others miss,
And this is the making of a Poetess!
Your feelings deep, and beauty glows,
Within your lovely soul!
So do not allow your self to falter,
Follow through and see the stars,
The Heavens, and the trees below,
The lakes and Rivers all aglow!
Others then will see your reflection in the mirror
on the snow.
Be Individual, find your door, and go through it.
Head held High! Look up, look up and see the sky!
Your words and phrases flying by.
Pick them up and write them down,
and never mind the laughing clowns!

SHADOWS

Were they just shadows on the wall?
    They rise and fall,
    They dance and play,
They never stay for long. You will never know
What the shadows think or say;
    They are sad, they are gay,
    But you will never know
    The shadows on the wall!
Laughter silent, silver grey,
    A tree, a bird,
    They tell no tales, but whom do they call—
Those shadows on the wall?

* * *

THE SILENT

There are the silent bits of heaven,
Catch them while you may.
    Some days are filled with sorrow,
    Interwoven with a ray of hope
That you may borrow for the little time you stay!
Your heart is in the wilderness, and the
    Wild winds you push away, until tomorrow;
    Then let it be a small memory in your gallery.
It is so hard to bear, but pick up the bits
Of Heaven in between and in the air.
    Be it summer sun or winter moon,
    Heaven is still there.
Your bits are in between,
Reach out and hold them far, and close to your heart today,
    And look upon the evening star.
    Let your painful thoughts flow to the sky
    And then you say goodbye.

Tomorrow, then a new horizon; laugh, be gay, and see the day.
All new and bright, even if the rain is there.
    Be not wrought, for it will wash your painful heart.
    Now the ebb and tide will flow,
    Be still my heart, and let me go!
But bring me back my lost and exquisite treasure.
I must soar cloud high, be free, be free!
    But let me be, oh! let me be!
    Let not my soul sleep the time away
    Life's stream be broken in the whirl and turmoil
    Of my heart.
I must not let the hurt hold me in its grip,
So I cannot advance. Oh, let me go! Oh, let me go!
    Let me find an alabaster cave, a silver vail,
    But I have no wings to fly.
    Let me then be a bird, then I shall be free
And I shall light on a willow tree!
Let me be a bird, I must not fall.
    Stand up, stand up and hear the call!
    My lost love.

THERE IS HOPE

Some may say our world is doomed, without amend, to have polluted air and dirty waters and hungry men, but surely somewhere there is hope.

Today I took a long walk. I saw a little robin making a nest so I stopped to talk. Mother Nature nodded that there is hope.

Down by the flooding cool stream, little fish swam in waters so fresh, untouched by careless human flesh, and I thought, yes, there is hope.

I saw a small child making sand castles by the seaside as the waves rolled with the tide. Let us work swiftly, while there is hope.

DIVINING LIGHT

Around me all is hush
Into the cold winter night,
While the heavenly virtue beams
With Beauty infinite.

Stir not, the blissful night
Mid the clear blue skies!
For I think I can understand
Why it has caught my eye!

How lovely, the world was made to be,
As poised upon its height
God bestows His trusting beams
To make the shadows bright.

Now, with varied thought
Of the blurred path of life,
Be thou my light, O thou Most High,
That I might shun the ways of strife?

One step higher every day,
Guided by the Heavenly Light!
For it is Thee who guidest best,
Through the day, or through the night.

O Light that sweeps the Night away,
My heart now fill
With love more perfect and of strength
Yielded to God—His bless'd Will.

RAMA

The Golden cow. . .
Child of the sacred calf. . .laughs in the dawn. . .
My love engulfed in myrrh and mist. . .
The scent. . .the quiet breath
Airplanes overhead. . .city hum. . .
Common reality. . .

A satin softness is my beloved;
As smooth as jasper
As scented as spring. . .
My love is Rama,
As ancient as the God of Darkness

Hunger. . .longing. . .
An eluding child of God's caprice is Mate-ism
How can two lovers change. . .
But always change together?

Why tongue?. . .Why education?
Oh, be a hedon. . .feel. . .

Like a lioness I lie in lair. . .
Await a look. . .a word. . .an intangible. . .
When life presents its opportunity
Do I know how to grab. . .to take. . .to caress it?
Open me wide. . .free. . .strong. . .
White light

Savor the morsels
A tasty repast at God's feast is life
The *pièce de résistance!*
The aperitif. . .the dessert cordial. . .
My beloved is the tasty pomegranate. . .

Many rooms has this white mansion
The rooms with Mato. . .well
He is. . .
Rama. . Faceted clear lake in the sunshine. . .
I can only see your face
When I see my own reflection in the pool. . .

My bower is green. . .earth's around. . .
Let me sleep and drift in your arms. . .
The ferns. . .our friends. . .the wood creatures. . .
My golden beloved, the gods heckle me
And show me your sweetness
So late in eternity. . .
Capricious devils. . .teach. . .
Don't taunt me with ridicule

Can't we be twins?

Mischievous one

I do. . .

(From the motion picture *Rama,* a story in visual poetry
of every human being from birth to death. Distributed by Film
Makers Co-op, N.Y.)

THE COMPANY MAN'S LOYALTY

The Company Man is quick to say,
"Give us your life, give us your pay;
Give us your body, and your mind too;
We'll take care of it, we'll take care of you."

The Company Man is intent on exchange,
He'll give you security, he'll give you some change;
He'll give you connections, he'll give you position;
He'll arrange your society, he'll provide you a physician.

The Company Man is magnanimous, a father ideal,
A paragon of virility and virtue, a eunuch of the real;
A preacher, a companion, a friend of family woe;
A protector, a sponsor, when your destiny demands you go.

A Company Man's omniscient, omnipotent, omnipresent, alack!
Omnivorous of all, ominous of naught, Amening to no one
Save the black of blue chips, and the market tips, and the
    red lips of his success;
Unaware of your soul, your taste, your freedom for
    difference.

The Company Man is nature and artifice, the sun and
    infinity;
The Company Man is colorless and fancy-free,
The Company Man is ignorant of love and truth,
The Company Man is a loyal servant of John Wilkes Booth.

* * *

THE BAD POLITICIAN

A hero who plants weeds in a graveyard and calls them
roses.

THE GOOD POLITICIAN

A leader who harvests the Wheat from all the people,
And walks with them in the Breath of life.

* * *

THE WHITE POLITICIAN

No greater tyrant exists than this monolith of fire
    and brimstone piss. . . .
A liar, a leech, a thug and a thief,
A swinger of doors, a devotee of wars,
A cheat for the privilege of serving his enslaved.
Two attributes he does possess:
He has the sense of sinning for the popularity of the masses,
And the knack for making passes at asses or girls with or
    without glasses;
His destiny is the doom of the local bar
With his cronies in the drink, smoke, and cachinnation of
the dark back room.

* * *

THE BLACK POLITICIAN

No greater piece of scum exists than this Black
Mephistopheles. . .
A driver, a jiver, a numbers writer. . .
A hustler of whores, a lover of male paramours,
One who can only reach the head in the bathroom.
Two qualities are his:
He has the capacity of a ward leader and the limitations
thereof;
He can be arbitrary and slick with Black folks,
And appealing and grovelling with White folks.
Lo! He can never represent all the people. . .
The select who achieve the Above.

THE WINDS OF AUTUMN

The winds of autumn are stirring—
Stirring among dead leaves.
Fidgety grackles are whistling;
Cold, gray clouds are riding the breeze.

The carefree summer is over
With its swimming and strolling and trips.
The snap and vigor of autumn
Puts firmness again in our lips.

We're off to a winter of conquest,
To a winter of work and of fun!
Here's a health to you and to me,
And a health to next summer's sun!

* * *

TO ONE WHO IS STILL YOUNG

Remember that, though he is gray,
He loved once, and may love still.
So with your words be not so bold,
For some may have the power to kill.

Think not, with your fresh young blood,
That you are the first to have loved and sung.
Gray hairs, wrinkled hands, have known
The caress of affection when young.

70

TO A MOTHER-IN-LAW

A strong, approaching star could
Whisk away the moon, the wise men say.
So can a husband draw your daughter
From her accustomed orbit away.

* * *

THE WOMAN I'LL LOVE

Somewhere a woman waits for me,
And oh, I desire her so!
A woman—feminine, adorable, free—
One I shall be proud to know.

What is the fate that keeps us apart
And sets my days on edge?
All I ask is a loving heart
That will make and keep a pledge.

And what is the pledge? Only this:
Always to be close by,
Sometimes to give a kiss,
Bravely to live and bravely die,
Without fear of the final abyss.

LOVE TO SHARE

The searching soul longs for peace unknown.
Seek, and you shall find by a silent prayer and a moment
of humbleness
into the night of doubt and despair.
Turn from the lonely road and you will find the fountain
of youth,
peace, harmony and joy.
Outstretched in God's hand is love to share.

HUMANITY CRIES OUT AND GOD ANSWERS

Listen to the roar of humanity.
                All are seeking, but do they find?
Their souls cry out for peace, and it is nowhere to be found.
                Happiness is wanted by all, but it is a most
difficult goal to achieve.
The Creator wants His creation to return to Him.

FISHIN' ON THE ALLAGASH

As a young kid along the Allagash, where the
trout are jumpin' high—I see a car from outa
state go swiftly passin' by—

They've come ta fish they says, with rod 'n
reel so fine, they's gonna clean the river
out, won't leave a fish of any kind.

I'm settin' there on the bank in my tattered
pants, and the mud caked on ma heels—I'm all
eyes as they unpack, and start talkin' in their
city spiel.

I just stay there where I wuz, lookin' out
at ma crooked pole, hook 'n worm both outa
sight, in ma favrit fishin' hole.

Ma expects a mess o' fish, fer supper ya see;
Paw is sleepin' off a drunk, so the ketch is
up ta me.

Well—them city fellers is awful busy, a few
feet up the bank, but pretty soon I get a bite and
give that pole a yank.

That trout wuz at least a foot n'a half and
jumped all through the grass—I pull the hook
outa his mouth, and toss it hind me back.

Oh, them fellers started castin' out, lines
nearly reachin' yonder shore—an' that big
boat n' engine, damn such a roar—

Well, them trout musta wanted ta laugh, cause
they never touch a fly, ya gotta use worms,
and ya gotta be mighty sly—it's a crafty lot,
these country fish, like us folks that's
standin' by. .

When ya come fishin' on these waters, there's
little ya'll need ta bring—a pot fer coffee,
a kittle fer beans—oh, and one other thing. .
No one cares about yer faded hat, or the
buttons off yer shirt, it's only the soul
that matters here—that's all there is to hurt.

SLAVE SHIP

High prowed Spanish ship, cruising at a lazy clip,
Riding silently on the swelling tide;
Flaunting your power on the solemn swell, a white-starched
sailing hell,
Square-rigged naval pride.
Stark against the rising moon, thrusting her hull, oak-hewn,
The slaver glides close to the shore.
Lofty masts point in scorn away from earth where men are born
And the angry breakers roar.

Silver shrouds of spider web thread her to the ocean bed
As she prowls sinister and bleak.
With empty maw she rides the ocean tides,
Stalking the living ebony the slavers seek.
A prison boat, with morbid pleasure she seems to gloat
And dip her bow in diabolic glee.
A malignant spirit, in her hold, peers out, devil-bold,
Scanning the sweep of the sea.

Captain Calvo, royal and rich, feels the miser's itch.
The yellow metal has enslaved this lordly peer!
His chains of gold from seeking men and for the slaver's pen,
And he knows another catch is near.
He's set the cruel snare—no man to spare,
For his heart's a thing of stone.
He and the men who man his spars are creatures of an avenging
Mars,
And the weary breakers moan.

In his cabin, inlaid with elephant bone, he plans alone:
With cunning the cargo can be had for free!
There're slaves ashore and there'll be countless more;
Just load and slip out to sea.
His crew of bearded drunks wallow in their bunks,
Glutting themselves on Barbados rum.
Calvo's mate, Reales, a treacherous swine, is not slave to
the vine
And he covets the Captain's plum.

Captain Calvo loads the hold but delays delivery of the gold
Through an act of arch deceit.
He gets a full cargo aboard without touching his yellow hoard
By a master criminal feat.
While Reales revels with the crew of sots, the Captain's
death he plots;
For perfidy he doesn't lack.
Three of the crew are completely out; the rest can get about,
When he drives his blade, hilt-deep, in the Captain's back.

"Curse the luck. Abandon ship. The plague has struck."
The shouted lie sets aflame each wine-addled brain.
Driven by fright in the dark of the night
Over the side they swarm—the drunken insane.
Over straining oars they row toward dark unknown shores
With thick-tongued curse.
The boats touch the sand and they rush madly inland
Forgetful of the golden purse.

Reales isn't in the clear even though land is far arear,
For on the horizon towering black clouds arise.
He curses his crew of three when twenty are needed in a
stormy sea
That flings salt spray in his eyes.
The wind shrieks in the shrouds and rain pours from the
clouds
As over the sea the ship is blown.
Coral covers her now from rotted stern to crumpled bow,
And the angry breakers groan.

THE WALL
(BERLIN)

Staunch and resolute, impregnable and fast,
Imprisoning the future and locking out the past;
A fortress made of metal, of cold and barren steel,
Unfriendly and unyielding; unable, too, to feel;
So many hearts are broken, hearts that will never mend,
With lover leaving lover, and friend deserting friend;
The cries of little children, the futile hopeless tears,
The agony of mortals in bondage to the years;
How long will you be standing, oh, morbid Wall of Doom?
How long will you imprison these people in your gloom?
We must have help from Heaven, as in the days of yore,
Come, Gabriel, and blow your horn, blow down the Wall once
more!

* * *

IT MIGHT HAVE BEEN

Bitter as the tears that fall as Death's sad, unbidden call is
answered by the One who was held nearest to the heart;
Cruel as the lashing whip, as its thunderous, roaring rip
Circles through the air until it finds its bloody mark;
Empty as the blackest night, tempest threatening, out of
sight
Every tiny star has hidden 'til the storm's mad rage is spent;
These but barely can convey the unfathomable dismay
Of that oft-repeated, musing phrase, "It might, it might
have been!"

MAD CYCLE

I never climbed Mount Everest,
Nor scaled an Alpine peak,
But I've roamed o'er the world,
To nurse the crippled and weak.

I've never been covetous
Of anyone's fame,
But I've always been jealous
Of my good name.

I never craved riches
Nor all the world's goods,
For I could find it all
By a walk in the woods.

The thorn in the rose—
I never queried why,
And behind barbed wire
I still saw the blue sky.

I saw pain in a mother's eyes
When her child begged for food;
I heard our captor's laughter
When he gave her the boot.

I have never seen peace,
Though cries of "Peace" fill the air;
While "cold wars" rage fiercely,
And victims cry with despair.

GREEN WHISPERS

Sleep, million-fingered giant,
Breathe lightly.

The wind caught in the long grass
Tears at the green hair of the world's skull.

The ants whisper:
The grass is envious,
It would embrace the sky.

Green hymn of adoration made
To the sun. Green incense growing.

When the sun rises
The wind is green.
The trees are splashed by wind
Into the color of grass.

Green is the prelude to summer:
The clouds mirror the grass.
The clouds take root.

HONEY CHILD

(A Mommy's Lullaby)

At the close of day across my way
I heard a voice singing soft and low,
A mommy trying to hush her baby's cries,
These are the words I often heard:

"Honey Child, don't cry, it's time to go,
It's slumber time and the sandman has called.
Rest your head upon my breast while
Mommie sings to you:

'Sweet Lullaby, Sweet Lullaby, Honey, don't cry.
Yes, Daddy will come home soon;
You are here in my arms.' "

She dimmed the lights and whispered low,
"Please Honey, it's time to go;
Yes, the angels keep watch all through the night.
Honey Child, go to sleep and goodnight."

That's a Mommy's Lullaby.

DREAMS

Dreams are spun of brightest silver
Long before we learn,
How to pick the threads of heaven
For a dream we spurned.

Heaven was too far away,
Time was closer by;
And as Life goes on and on
We no longer try.

Never do we weave like spinners,
Only you and I
Sadly turn and watch beginners
As they bravely try.

Weave one dream and then relinquish
All the ones you had;
Keep it safe, and when it's finished
They'll be all you have.

For the keeping, for the keeping,
Is the treasured past;
Keep it safe for all your dreaming
Then let go at last.

For a dream is but a vision
Of some time that's past,
And will never come again
Because it was the last.

AFRICAN TALKING DRUMS

Open wide the tropical gate,
And get inside my mate;
I'll be your only friend,
Where sweet Sunshine transcends.
In endless joy in Afric's soil,
The heart awaken with its toil.
My drums sound to ring,
On that darling feet I'll sing.

Open that gate of grace,
And see my black face;
Under the Moon, to Sea abroad,
The treasures of arts in every land.
Of talking drums, of chicken art,
With its charm and stream running heart;
Yonder I'll sit on that green grass,
In the tropical stark of brass.

Take me abroad, I'll cry;
Open the gate I'll glorify;
In black soil to ocean unknown,
For the talking drum is my own
For the Kings and Savants to see,
The greater power of music run so free.
My talking drums I'll play,
From the sweet old, old lay.

I know my right under the tropical Sun,
With its bliss and grace from the Moon;
I'll caress in that sweet moment,
With the songs of love, never to lament.
Under the Moon, in jungle tract,
My talking drum brings the fact;
In that realm I'll remain,
Free from bondage and its chain.

Let me talk my drum to claim,
Under the palm tree of its game;
With the tongue so high,
Through the desert I'll walk and sigh,
And sing and wabble under the tree,
With my drums inspiring free.
To all mortal land I'll stand,
With my drums of command.

There's joy behind the river,
Off the ocean far from Lucifer;
Away from the cave of pauper,
I'll be the only talking drummer
To wake your heart of art,
Sweet in hamlet to the Desert.
To East and West with talking drum,
I'll meet my only chum.

I'll talk and hum with the faithful,
With donors, hovers, admirers and beautiful;
My talking drums will open that gate,
To dance with the host and mate.
Jump up and cry up, in voices of mission,
Of joy enfold, manifest in creation.
Under the cool weather of sweet fruit
I'll beat my drum and long flute.

I'll stand in this palmy sand,
With the echo of drum and band;
With the echo, like dreams to win,
The trodden heart so lost in sin.
I'll hear from morn to sunset,
Under the blue sky of lofty minaret.
Listen then, the fanfare and drum,
To dance with drum and chum.

If here I'm wrong forgive me,
For my talking drum is free;
To twist dancers and optimist,
And say I'm the only artist
Whose band play with the wise,
For I support the best enterprise;
To amuse with this happy property,
For talking drums is fair property.

I'll close the gate or open it,
In its realm of love and wit;
I'll ride on horseback with my lyre,
Decorated with drums and native attire
To claim that world from abyss,
Where my songs bring its bliss.
To many on earth that work will show,
Light of joy, to many lands flow.

LOVE THY NEIGHBOURS

God has built this beautiful world,
With the banner of love unfurled;
And enjoins us to live and labour,
In harmony with our neighbour.

He who splits shall languish and cry,
In sorrows that love and peace deny;
But he who loves his neighbour shall see,
Grace abundant in love that be.

Every day the Sun passes this way,
With its glowing light and splendour;
Transporting our love and candour,
Wherein our hearts forever display.

We shall live and see the flowing tide,
Great waters and ocean on every side;
In joy all created will flow like neighbours,
In restless hours in their harbours.

Hate not thy neighbour, but help
Those in need of friendly hands;
Wake in courage and moral strength,
And help thy neighbour as love commands.

Fear not where enemies stand
To break thy spirit, yet command;
Fight like heroes in the strife,
Of undaunted spirit in daily life.

Swear not with the arrogant tongue,
Who've lost grace in life's long run;
Love shall build the world anew,
Where neighbours shall live as one.

Spare no moment to conspire or cry,
And salvation, never, never deny;
But show the spirit of manhood to brave,
Difficulties that rend the heart to grave.

Life has wisdom, love and passion,
To outlive mortal right and mission;
In bounteous yoke to wake our love,
With the gracious hands of Angels above.

Life has great moments for love,
Where unchanging hearts never move;
To help the needy from sins of omission,
With earthly perversion and remission.

Love thy neighbour as thyself,
Is a pillar where blessing descends;
Everyday, as we put our trust in Him,
Whose Love, success in life depends.

Leave not your heart to the sorrow,
Or temptation that comes with tomorrow;
But pray in time of need and plenty,
HELP—and your love upon others empty.

EDUCATION, LEARNING, GROWTH

Educo means, "lead out of"!
Students teach through desire, love!
We are e'er learning in life,
In and out of class through strife!
We learn through what we like most!
Often retain what pained most!
Through suff'ring, for Self we search!
Self's Temple is our true Church!
For poor, don't deny the group!
Good works through life's varied loops!
If we're happy when we learn
To more Education turn!
Voyages into the past,
Education's life's true mast!
If we can motivate them,
Knowledge we won't seam and hem!
Each situation conveys,
Messages through all our days!
If we find pupils' int'rest,
We guide their direction best!
Good or bad from us observed;
Ill actions, feelings be curbed;
Then good names we've deserved!
Let good teaching overrule!
We'll have good credentialed schools!
Anguished sadness won't perturb;
Students, teachers, know more verve!
Our well-trained hearts and skilled minds,
In Education's Halls find!
Those who care and truly try,
Indiff'rence won't us defy!
Trickery tries to fool youth!
We'll find good answers in truth!
Good teachers dedicated,
To truth are predicated!

Good service gladly will yield;
Although varied be our field!
Humbly learn to give pupils
Courage to face truth's scruples!
Education instructs them,
Lighting int'lect's diadem!
Whether professionally
Heart trains feelings, attitudes;
Mind trains our good thoughts' etudes!
Scholars, teachers interchange,
Ability rearrange!
Learn from students, turnabout!
Humble professors reroute!
Patience is our guiding light!
Arrogant ego's our blight!
Higher mind will educate,
Compassion's our learning mate!
Love finds answers mind can't find!
Lower self it does refine!
Its ability's limitless,
Depending on receptiveness!
Trained or just factually,
We all teach one another!
Be good sister and brother!
If mental maturity yearns,
Control self from lower turn!
No harsh opression we'll know!
Mind and heart balancedly flow!
Gentle self restrain we gain,
As from hostility abstain!
We don't just give but receive!
Education won't deceive!
Don't just refrain from impulse;
Forbearance choose; don't repulse!
Lower self is our trial!
Learning's not just denial!
Good ideas we substitute;

Replacement's our tribute!
It blesses both: The donor,
Receiver, feel the honor!
Thus dedicated people
Raise Education's steeple!
Reverence, appreciation—
Belong in Education!
Darwin's theory we now know!
Nature evolved, who will show?
We feel free to questions ask,
Thus enriching each one's task!
Don't let's fear mistakes!
Wisdom walks through Inner Halls;
Digested knowledge's recalled!
True Living is real exam!
Wisdom we've found we can't cram!
Let's truly study feelings,
In good thoughts find our healings!
We have learned only "a truth,"
In Spirit's world we're a youth!
The more we learn, we then see,
How limited we can be!
Wisdom's Horizon's Self's Scope!
Vast realms we don't know, but hope!
Eternal mentality!
It's a Reality!
Limitless, Love's vital flow,
Great Benevolence "They" Know!
In enrichment we'll partake!
Constantly we'll overcome,
Education is never done!
Growing's good for every one;
Though painfully we have won!
Each blesses the other's work;
Thus good growth we do not shirk!
Education gladly turn,
Higher Self we won't now spurn!

Throw off limited shackles;
With lower self we grapple!
What was a problem now find,
Good answers in Higher Mind!
Higher heart will bring us peace!
God's True Loving will release!
We often fear the unknown!
Security, Faith's answer's tone!
"Patience" is our growth's key word!
Both students and teachers heard!
We'll know good education,
In or out situation!
Formal or informal schools,
Is how we learn Self's true rules!
Is it "hang up" or excuse,
To let lower self run loose?
Listen to Self's direction!
Spirit's our real protection!
We can't repeat too often,
Humble growth does us soften!
Insightfullness we'll learn,
Inspiration helps discern!
Those overweighted in mind,
Lower self's emptiness find!
The overweighted in heart,
Need calm thoughtfulness to start!
Higher self's not in a book,
Thoughts from good books help us look!
Until for true self we search,
Lower self leaves us in lurch!
On Inner Planes we find sages;
True education's pages!
Blessed Wisdom, Love, Patience,
Balance Inner World's Radiance!
Our growth so many have helped,
Many we've not seen but felt!
Spirit's Presence we don't see,

Nor atomic energy!
Glorious Hosts ever be;
Helping us impartially,
Advancing eternally!
Learning's growth truly look,
Find Self in strong, quiet nook!
Spirit's unseen pinnacle,
Love, Truth's constant miracle!
Sages wait for us to ask;
Humility helps us in life's task!
Impersonal inspiration,
Through each Self's dedication!
Growth, in physical have zones
Hear Inner Freedom's true tones!
Even those who can't afford,
Find ways of earning reward!
Trickery hears mental groans,
Truth and Beauty grow as loans,
We repay for others' aid!
As for us others have paid!
Books in paperbacks do sell;
Inspiring thoughts they tell!
Freedom's ways we choose,
There are good reasons for our laws!
Arrogance can't see our flaws!
Fog's only temp'rary sight!
Spirit and Self shed the Light!
Enemies abuse the laws,
Justice has its mighty saws!
Liberty's Halls inspire,
Enlightenment's attire!
Knowledge's magnificent!
But Wisdom's omnipotent!
Turn to prayer or meditate;
Thus our true Self we'll locate!
Education's Inner Halls,
Skillfully we'll hear the calls!

Weak licentious ways won't use!
Reverse of democracy,
Is forced rule's autocracy!
Negativity lights fuse,
For lower self to misuse!
Trickery of intellect,
Spirit will help us detect!
Eagerly to Self let's turn,
Mighty lessons we will learn!
Knowledge we'll truly digest,
Thus Self's wisdom's our bequest!
Our freedom goodness protects;
Oppression loses effects!
Effort placed on how to learn;
Now no vandalisms burn!
Destructiveness let's refuse;
Good growth, patience we will choose!
PRACTICE helps us climb Self's hill
Idleness doesn't gain skills!
We realize need for laws;
To protect from human flaws!
Then some structure we do need!
Indifference no lasting creed!
Not overemphasis see,
Checks, balances, keep us free!
Freedom's Education's seed,
Slick rhetoric's no retort,
Light from Self's our worthy port!
Through debating we can know,
Mental agility show!
We can prove or disprove thought,
Heart's answers in Self we've sought!
Freedom allows minds attract,
Through loving laws we'll come back!
We'll overcome prejudice,
Now we'll learn to live 'Justice'!
Growth is true choice of the free;

Not low mental slavery!
Shun emotional bondage,
As we increase Inner Sage!
Have a True Light's Renaissance!
True Self knows our circumstance!
To protect us from dark greed!
Standards let's truly see,
But without rigidity!
By prayer and meditation
Find God in all Creation!
Humility helps us know,
Halting arrogance's flow!
If there is a course to take,
Requirement don't forsake!
Patience awaits silently,
Humility greets quietly,
More gentility we find,
Greater courage is its kind!
Good language lets us choose,
Our deepening growth, Self's infuse!
Through loving humor control,
Lower self kindly parole!
If we forgive our own faults,
We'll rise above small self's vaults!
Realism now we free;
Idealism's harmony!
Darkness slowly, really fades,
Beauty's, Truth's hues it can't shade
Elegance will always live!
Wrong sifts through our Self's sieve
We find growth worth the effort;
The pen's mightier than sword!
Freedom's Love-Truth's reward!
Great leaders of the ages,
Turned to vast Inner Sages!
Great brains cannot a tree make!
Explain real cause of earthquake?

Hurricane's fury we know,
But true causes can we show?
Mentality they do shake!
Egotism let's forsake!
There are deeper reasons for freaks;
Answers find if we seek!
Not just through mind, but belief!
Enlightenment's our True Sheath!
Others growth we now support!
Our fear is what truly hurts,
True Faith, so hard to assert,
Good in all lands, we plead,
Join to overcome dark greed!
What's really Nature And Man??
Masters help, Choice is our span!
Free will is our conscious growth;
Voluntarily, good showeth!
Then we're really, truly freed,
For more new growth's now our creed!
Great Leader, born in stable;
Wise men know it's not fable!
Patient service Lord has known;
Great kindness He has shown!
Ancient Egypt was advanced;
Surfaces we've only glanced!
Nothing new under the "Son"!
Let's search for Self, everyone!
All religions try for good,
If we truly understood!
Orthodoxy knows rigidity,
Spirit flows to all freely!
We must earn Spirit's reward,
Then growth's truly an award!
Reconverted energy,
Man, though programmed Mentally,
Love, free choice dumps memory!
Spirit knows not density;

94

Consciousness, immensity!
Programming reactive mind,
Answer what's o'er mind? God find!
Through mind-hearts balance become;
Better understanding's done!
Thus egocentricity,
Falls prey to autocracy!
Arise to Self and Spirit,
Lovely melody, hear it?
Bless our youth, bless our ages!
True growing is in stages!
Who can doubt all history's facts?
Some are lies, but truth's intact!
Is part of Eternity!
Silent Watchers give credit!
Growth of self can't be debit!
Checks and balances need be;
It's a fact from history!
Mental arrogance we find,
Limits inspiration's blind!
Emotional's bold, can't be told
We set our limited hold!
Our Self's cradles true growth's climb!
Free will comes with practice, time!
Upon our Faith we depend,
Then true learning we defend!
"Living's" our wisest school,
If we search for learning rules!
Positive's good attitude,
Leads us seek true, not rude!
Our negatives will swirl out,
As we make good turnabout!
Know lower self's not power,
We'll climb good Self's high tower!
As we trip up Mastery's Hill,
Spirit helps lift our will!
True living is our learning;

To more knowledge we're turning!
It's up to us to believe,
Before we really achieve!
Words' mystery ship docks in port,
Shedding light through loving thought!
On Words feasts, festively dine;
Thought's pageantry's heady wine!
Thoughts, feelings, prejudices clear!
Minds and hearts empty of fear!
Lest Higher Self we betray,
Words eloquence, delightful spray!
Mem'ry colors Flowers Hill,
Loving words are Life's windmill!
Joy's fluted thoughts words echo!
Peace is resounding, "Hello!"!
Verbal feelings, music's flow,
Words thoughtful rainbow's aglow!
When thoughtless words we assert,
Pray guard thoughts from petty dirt
Before careless words we blurt!
Gracious gifts from Self's friend;
Cheerful thoughts through voices send!
Atmosphere they permeate,
True Self we'll now radiate!
Inner Self's e'er reflected!
Gentleness, words protected!
People receive our first row,
As Spirit's symphony will flow!
True Beauty now's selected!
Lies' ugliness detected!
If our life we've to defend,
Self Word's Power will us send!
Cruel, harsh thoughts—feelings flee!
Hearts-minds' True Word healers be!
Caref'ly words are selected,
Self's Wisdom's now reflected!
Self's Mind and Heart we've married!

Right attitudes words have carried!
Now our actions and words show,
Words are liars' deadly foe!
Speech's darkness, turn to right!
Relax and tensions lose their might!
Inner Self's expressed in Word!
Greetings' friendly Voice is heard!
Clean minds' and hearts' pollution. . .

* * *

FROM ECOLOGY OF SPIRIT

WHAT IS JUSTICE IN AMERICA?

What is justice in this land of the free?
Is it the same for you and for me?
In the halls of justice, is it how you are dressed,
Or the noted lawyer by which the jury is impressed?
Is justice for the rich and the poor,
Or the name you have on your door?
Is it the same for the man who labors in a ditch,
Or is it just for doctors, policemen, and the rich?
If a policeman is accused of a crime,
The court is for him all the time.
He is acquitted and the judge will
Shake hands with the policeman still.
A doctor is accused of a crime; he tells of the wrongs he
has done;
The court ignores his deeds, another victory he has won.
How many more will suffer by his hand?
When is a crime not a crime in this great land?
A poor man has his day in court,
There is no justice, for his sort,
He is found guilty; his chances were slim,
And you don't see the judge shaking hands with him.
Is the jury attentive all through the day,
Or are their thoughts so blurred that
Some of the facts are not even heard?
You enter the court room, you see the scale,
And you hope and pray that you will prevail.
Soon you sense the doom,
You know there is no justice in that room.
The scale of justice you have seen in vain,
And for you, there will be no need to enter again.
Are all men created equal in this day and time?
Does it make a difference who committed the crime?
What is justice in getting an appeal?
To the poor, it doesn't seem real.
The costs are unjust.

What do you do? In what do you trust?
What is justice in the printing of news?
Is it your name, your social standing, that determines the
views?
Are the truths printed about the rich, too,
Or are they more privileged under the red, white and blue?
You may be a doctor, a policeman, or have a name on your door,
As for me, I am amongst the very poor.
The biased news I have read, and in the courts I saw
They have abolished the constitutional law.
Is justice the same for you and for me?
Is this the land of the free?
Are all men created equal, as they were meant to be?

* * *

NO ONE CARED

A man was lying in the street,
People were standing at his feet,
They talked, they said that he was dead,
No one offered to check his head.
He is a nobody, he is nothing to us,
Why should we make a fuss?
If he is dead, nothing is solved;
If he is not, we won't be involved.
We will go away, and leave him alone,
We have no conscience, we will never atone.
In our minds we surely are right,
Why fret, if he has lived his last night?
He is a stranger, the man in the street,
He will never be standing at our feet.
No one helped him, they didn't dare;
No one helped, they didn't care.

THE REASON WHY. . .

When I saw you at first,
You were in my eyes
Like all my acquaintances.
There was really
Not any difference between them and you.
A little later I noticed your wisdom,
I noticed your least virtue;
Your heart attracted my heart.
Ever since then you won my esteem.
Yes, you thrill and rouse my heart
Which inundates you with love and sweetness.
It is not a thunderbolt.
Certainly you have made it out;
Surely you have felt it.
I love you more and more.
I consider you much because you are kind.
You always give and hopelessly give yourself.
I trust you because you are honest and loyal.
I admire you because you are full of charm;
You are sweet, noble, peaceful, industrious,
Patient, upright, generous, meticulous;
Because you are an ideal person:
Your goal is always success,
Success in anything you undertake.

Myrtha B. Corbier

I cherish you because your character doesn't skim
The barbarism and the vulgarity;
Because you can discern the good and the evil.
I appreciate you because you differentiate
The humility from the flattery,
The prudence from the fright,
The disinterestedness from the idiocy,
The self-control from the silliness,
The loyalty from the selfishness,
The devotedness from the ostentation,
The reserve from the apathy.
You are not taken in by appearances,
And you don't confuse
The simplicity and the ugliness,
The tranquility and the timidity.
I esteem you because you distinguish
The perseverance from the obstinacy,
The perspicacity from the susceptibility,
The firmness from the hardness,
The recreation from the debauchery,
The love from the sentimentality,
The enthusiasm from the extravagance,
The thriftiness from the miserliness,
The liberality from the prodigality,
The dexterity from the malice,
The mercy from the casualness,

The character from the look.
Obtuseness! Tyranny! You react wisely;
You evoke for their producer: pity, favor, pardon;
You provide some verses stressing a suitable lesson.
The crowd doesn't affect your logic judgment;
Your experiences help you
Not only look at the quantitative value.
O sagacity! O stillness! Any intimacy unbalances them.
Your keen personality makes you sound with accuracy
Even the more likely testimony about your neighbor;
And you don't misinterpret his thought.
You find it flat to dim his attributes
At the profit of your own enhancement.
You are a child as regards the humility,
And a man as for the reasoning.
Your nature doesn't differ from the human's,
But your permanent and recorded struggles immunize you
Against the unbridled attack of your flesh.
Your actions are identical with your language,
Which is as exquisite as the honey.
O my heart, it is palpitating strongly!
My body is trembling, my eyes are overjoyed,
And then, all my being is in rapture.
In short, I love you because you love God,
And He takes pleasure in you.
I love you again
Because you contribute to my glee and bliss.

ANCIENT TRUST

As man extends his mastery of earth,
He bears himself as would a tyrant king,
Imagining an ordained right of birth
To subjugate and ravish everything.
Amid his zeal to fill his appetite,
To seize, pervert, and trample Nature down,
Does he forget that what he deems a right
Is not the trust that won for him his crown?
That ancient trust involved a keeper's care
To tend the base of life by which he rose,
Neglecting which he may himself despair,
Lost from the vital will to which he owes
All that he is, all he can ever be—
His own ascent to world supremacy.

* * *

OCTOBER MOON

October's nights will match its sunlit days
In splendor and cathedral majesty
On those rare evenings when, with magic rays,
The harvest moon lights up the canopy.
For then the moonbeams seem to strike the ground
Like ghostly rain, all bouncing into air
Whose bracing stillness amplifies the sound
Of crickets and a barking dog, that share
The quiet with the distant murmuring
Of human voices. The enchanted night
Gives vague and fancied shapes to everything
Kissed by the unseen sun's reflected light,
Whose faraway influences suggest
To mankind that the time has come for rest.

MARCH WINDS

March winds are blowing, brisk and strong,
        Messengers of spring.
Buds are swelling, blossoms bursting,
        Winter has taken wing.
Ice and snow shall fade away.
Welcome spring, and long delay.

Loud gusts roar in the vacant trees,
        Heave at the window pane.
Clouds are gathering, dark and threatening;
        Thunder, sweeps of rain.
Ice and snow no more appear.
Winter's gone and spring is here.

* * *

THE BIRTHDAY GIFT

A pretty little blue-eyed girl
Displayed a bracelet on her wrist.
Though made of brass, it matched her curl,
And, too, her rounded, dimpled fist.

Her babbling baby laughter told
Much more than words could do, how she
Was glad to get, when two years old,
This handsome gift of jewelry.

A trinket only, yet her arm
Gave it a beauty that no gem
Could have possessed, a grace and charm
Deriving from the seraphim.

Winifred M. Cowie

THE FASCINATING SEA

O, Come with me by the side of the sea,
We will tread thru the soft gray sand,
Watching the waves dash merrily,
Coming up nearer the land.

Look at the seagulls as they fly by,
Squawking and darting thru the sky.
Overhead is a canopy of azure blue,
With fleecy clouds floating thru.

A wealth of mystery lies on the shore,
Small stones of all colors and sea shells galore.
Let us stop and gaze at the beautiful sight—
The sunny sky, dancing waves are a delight.

The billowing whitecaps rolled and dashed,
At last they achieved their goal—the land.
They washed away sand piles and castles were smashed
As they came up dancing on the sand.

The golden rays of the summer sun
Shines down and adds a glow,
To go out by the sea is so much fun
Both old and young folks know.

CANON MOUNTAIN   1937

We were on vacation time
To New Hampshire we did go;
Lafayette campsite was just fine
It was a place we wanted to go.

We set up our tents in a suitable spot
And quickly unpacked our supplies,
We started the campfire—food was our thought—
It seemed practical and wise.

The campfire burning in the dark,
It was a delightful scene,
And we nestled in our mountain nest
The mountain around us made it seem.

From the light of the moon we got a good view
of Canon Mountain tramway,
And a silhouette of the Old Man of the Mountain, too,
His rocky magnificence in display.

Under the starlit sky
We sat around the log fire;
We sang and talked of our desire,
To climb Canon Mountain we would try.

We retired to our tents and slept,
In the morning our promise we kept
To awake in the morning full of zip,
Ready to start on our mountain trip.

We ate breakfast, packed a lunch
Perhaps we would get hungry, that was our hunch.
We started to ascend the mountain trail,
Our thoughts of success seemed to prevail.

106

Often the trail was rough and steep,
We would crawl over rocks at times,
The children never thought of defeat,
Anticipation later was in their minds.

We arrived at Canon Mountain landing and ate our lunch;
The passengers had just arrived in the tram car.
They were astonished seeing our youthful bunch,
And that we had come so far.

We started down after we rested a bit,
Full of enthusiasm and joy.
It was dark when we arrived at our campsite,
But the brilliant moon and sparkling stars
Were there for us to enjoy.

DEATH, STEP BACK

Death, walk back a little way,
Do not follow so close behind me.
Give me another autumn, another spring.

Another spring that I may see once more
The earth and rain and sun and air
Unite to give the miracle of birth.
Look where the offsprings come!
New little leaves of grass,
And tender leaves on shrubs and trees;
That is only a glimpse.

Then I will wait for autumn,
With cricket songs and peaceful days,
With harvest and the turning of the leaves—
Red and yellow, gold and brown,
And lingering bits of green.
Prodigal beauty, and generous yield of crops!
Beloved fall time!

Death, go back a step or two,
Take up your shadow.
Give me another spring, another autumn.

SPRING POEM

in the biogenesis—
   i beheld the elegant eros of egrets
   courting their narcissistic mates,
   pirouetted
   on the flesh film of the rhombic river,
   i felt the chanson of the
   hummingbirds' wings whisper
   into ecstasies of sonic shivers,
   and was humbled by the omnipotent
   energy of the sun genesis
   where, refracted, the scintillations
   Of radiant nova in my eyes,
   they began to bleed light
   profusely—
       a spectroscopic maelstrom
   swirling-swimming in the eyeball,
   encompassing the circumference
   of the atomic all.
   while the god neutron polarized
   into the proton of the man
   and the electron of the beast—
   a fusion into the fecundity
   of consummated mergence.
in a light-star near,
an agonizing spasm—
then convolutes,
gestating the fetus of the
       enigmatic Emergence.

EVOLUTION

i bloomed in both
baneberry and bud,
and i broke bread
in the bloody bed of birth.
i bled in belief,
believing
the broken bone of the
baptism of the becoming;

in the blood of the bud,
i became.

* * *

THE GOD-MOUNTAIN

this
mountain
is my
metaphysics,
born
of its
breach
and
broken balustrades,
a bishop's bastille
climbed in conflict,
where in the
cathedral of its crags
i was christened.

THE OSPREY

in the
symphony of the wind
the osprey
opens her orchestra
with the
baton of her beak,
raised and rising
to the flashing
of flesh and feathers
she flies filled
with her
forefathers' fever;
still fevered
she grasps the green gauntlet
with
claws of crimson
to rest as a
silhouette in the sun.

* * *

SINEW

the single sinew sews
our fiber into
plural knots of fire.

THE ALPS

I'd like to climb the Alps of faith,
  Of love and joy and peace,
To higher plains—to gain the heights—
  On life's best joys to hold a lease!
But if I wander all alone
  It's way beyond my reach,
So hand in hand I'll walk with you—
  See life unfold and teach!

I'd like to climb the Alps of faith,
  With someone who is true,
Who believes in me and shares my thoughts
  In whate'er I say or do!
And knows however dark the path,
  That faith will light the way
To greener fields and bluer skies—
  Where I shall sing a lighter lay!

I'll never falter as I go
  For I shall always see—
However rugged, rough the road,
  The implicit faith you have in me!
And whether I go up or down,
  Where'er my pathway lies—
I'll steadily go on and on—led by
  The shining faith in your eyes!

I'd like to climb the Alps of love,
  Of ectasy and bliss!
To feel the touch of your hand—
  The thrill of your kiss!
To see love grow and glow
  As I worship at its shrine,
And know contentment in the years
  If you were truly mine!

And so with faith and love comes joy—
    And peace of mind and heart,
Fulfillment of life's sweetest dreams—
    If each one does his part!
And as the years go on and on
    The Alps, as you will see—
Are not hard at all to scale—
    If you but walk with me.

* * *

THINKING THROUGH

A few minutes a day
    With our thoughts in array—
The cobwebs will clear
    From our mind and our soul,
And if we keep searching
    We'll soon reach the goal!
And upward and onward
    Strive for the right—
For others—ourselves
    By our God-given light!

LONELINESS

Have you ever been so lonely
   That you thought nobody cared,
And the world seemed sort of vacant and
   It made you kinda scared?

And you knew that no one loved you—
   Besides your friends, of course;
While you simply sat and wondered
   Why you felt such deep remorse.

When all at once you thought about
   Some folks worse off than you;
Then suddenly you felt ashamed—
   They could be lonely, too.

* * *

THE DATING GAME—YEAR 2000

Had a date with dame 708,
   But she said I'd have to wait.
Instead she went with 894
   Who's known to be a perfect bore.

Then I called up 459
   Answering service was on the line.
Phoned 3rd ex-wife 603;
   Said she'd spend some time with me.

Had great fun at Club 31
   Until the rising of the sun;
Now I know that 603
   Is number one again with me.

114

MOON MEN

When we were young we talked about
   The man upon the moon;
Little did we ever think
   It would happen quite so soon.

That men could fly, or go that high
   Were still "ifs" "ands" or "buts,"
And to even think they could
   Was considered just plain "nuts."

But conquer space—we did, of course—
   And landed on the moon;
'Twas hard to realize the fact
   That our two planets were in tune.

We brought back rocks and left some stuff,
   But just to keep things buzzin',
Not only did we send one man—
   We had to send a dozen.

As time goes on in future years,
   Mankind will have to say—
The astronauts who landed first
   Were from the U. S. A.

THE RULE OF THE ROOST

High in the hills of Tennessee
Lives a family by the name of Jeb and Sandy Lee.
They have a small flock of chickens and a bay hound dog,
A cow or two, and a single hog.
"Our rooster is gone," Ma said to Pa.
"Randy is jest away visiting," Pa said to Ma.
So Jeb took his hound dog and went out to plow,
Ma fed the chickens and tended the cow.
Sandy counted her chickens, and there were six—
She had called them by name ever since they were chicks.
Maisy and Daisy—Polly and Dolly—Lucy and Ruthie.
These six old biddies supplied them with eggs,
They were plump and healthy, with big, meaty legs.
The hens ruffled their feathers and strutted and scratched,
They clucked and cackled and shoved and snatched.
Then the first old biddy by the name of Maisy,
Pecked her rival by the name of Daisy.
Daisy stopped scratching, and pecked pretty Polly.
Polly gobbled a worm and pecked poor Dolly.
Dolly looked dazed and fought with Lucy.
Lucy flipped her wings and chased pert Ruthie.
This social-pecking order soon came to an end,
And there was silence again in the chicken pen.
Then Pa and the hound dog came 'round the bend.
"Great Caesar! The rooster has just crowed. . .he's near the
gate.
There's a jug of raw mash whiskey, let's celebrate!
Maisy is next—she's old and tough: she pecks and pushes,
she's awful rough."
So Maisy was simmerend into a tasty stew, flavored with
lots of Jeb's home brew.
Now Daisy is queen of the chicken pen—'til Pa and Ma have
stew again.

Mary M. Del Tedesco

AN AUTUMN TREE

Red, yellow, green, and brown,
These were the colors in her gown,
Nature's hand as an artist rare,
Painted here—dabbed there.

Her friend the Sun her cheeks did kiss,
For a while all was heavenly bliss,
Then came a knight with a stately prance,
And asked Her Majesty if she might dance.

Off with a hop, and over with a dip,
Elegantly she danced her part of her trip,
But when her friend the Sun did go,
This stately Prince was just a foe.

As he whistled and jerked at a maddening pace,
The poor autumn tree lost all her grace,
And when the Prince Charming bid her good day,
She was stripped of her gown, needless to say.

With arms outstretched and body bare,
All beauty gone—no one to care,
With frozen tears and hidden fate,
She waited for Spring to make a date.

GREECE'S EARLY DAYS

The Islands of the Aegean Sea
   Were the cradle of Greek art.
Can you feel yourself there now
   Searching for the long-lost key?

Ripple on the water meant wavy lines
   When winds were blowing over it,
And spiral lines stood for the twist of shells
Or the coils of climbing vines.

Down the road to art in the Aegean age,
   We travel far before we learn
That life in the Old World
   Moved along at a slow pace.

The first designs on pottery of that day
   Were all in cameo white or black;
Actually it was a kind of chalk
   Pressed into furrows cut into clay.

Then came designs of blossoms; grasses and reeds very tall
   Were depicted skillfully in dark colors;
In the light ground, the lily, the crocus and the iris,
   Shells, corals and sea urchin venerated by all.

Outlines of wall paintings in the great Palace of Knossos
   Were fine and strong and in lively colors;
Portraits of dancing girls, and boys bearing gold and silver
     cups,
   And a gentle scene of a child with a vase gathering crocus.

A favorite sport for acrobats was flying o'er the back
   Of a bull, or catching his grey horns;
Those cruel bull-grappling scenes on the palace wall
   Were painted by artists who saw them in the act.

In all the frescoes where there were women and men,
  Both have slender squeezed-in waists;
The artists wanted to make a distinction
  So she is painted white and he with brownish skin.

That civilization flourished for fifteen centuries;
  Sadly the ruins of Knossos were swept by fire in a vast
      overthrow;
Archaeologists divide the age in three Minoan periods
  And Bronze Age culture became dim memories.

* * *

TONIGHT

The orange moon hangs high and bright
  And enchanting stars are blue;
Soft shadows play on the quiet lagoon
  Beloved, I miss you tonight.

The trade winds sing a familiar tune
  While the bugle bird sleeps in the tree;
The wise white owl and the bumble bee
  Tell me that you see the same moon.

The imparadised hill I tread in delight—
  Where blossoms in their dewy slumber
Illume the pathless earth of calcined umber—
  Beloved, I miss you tonight.

ESPAÑA

Dear Spain, you are so far away
    I cannot see your sky,
But I hold you in my heart
    As the lark soars on high.

Your castles of great beauty and evergreens
    And winding rivers I adore,
Your olive trees, sweet dates and palms,
    And peaceful art colonies along the shore.

Dear Spain, if only I could be
    In beautiful Madrid in the old Prado,
I'd gaze in awe and be at ease
    With Goya's art of long ago.

Beautiful Spain—here were Kings of Aragon
    Peter the Third and Alfonso,
James, Martin, and John the First,
    And the art of Velasquez and El Greco.

Historical Spain, where Ferdinand and Isabella
    Were proclaimed king and queen;
They curbed the power of Henry the Fourth
    In Seville a House of Trade was seen.

Unforgettable Spain, your empire rose
    And you lived in glory in 1492,
Your power was Europe's strongest
    When Columbus sailed the ocean blue.

Dear Spain, for centuries that followed
    Eons of grandeur and gold were your legend.
Alas! Progress at last sadly ended
    Because of Charles the Fifth and Philip the Second.

AUTUMN

Did you ever walk—in the pale moonlight—
in majestic silence—with someone at night?—
do you ever feel—that the stars above—are
something that's needed—in your garden of love?—
do you ever stroll—beneath towering trees—
where soft shadows play—on multi-colored leaves?—
do you search for pretty blossoms—that line the
winding trail—that nature has painted—in balance
and detail?—the crimson, gold, and green—with little
thorns all there—and the glistening dew on the petals—
has made them all the more fair—do you merrily
roam—to sweet clover beds—where purple blossoms grow—
and the four-leaf clover spreads?—where the trill of the
sparrow—or the song of the lark—is awe-inspiring—
like magic in the dark—do you feel lonely and in despair—
where moonlight fades away—and twinkling stars have
gone to sleep—and dawn brings on a new day?—in
all fond dreams—have faith my dear friend—till storm
clouds pass—and AUTUMN comes again.

EXPLORE

I wander into this old barn,
Cobwebs hanging like dusty yarn.
The sun pours through the weathered boards;
Sparrows act as the castle lords.
They leave their trail everywhere,
They fly about without a care,
But the songs they sing show it more.
Towards the back there is no door;
Through it I see a field of mud,
Patches of weeds without a bud,
A row of silhouetted trees
That stand still and bare in the breeze.
Again I roam about inside;
I see a long forgotten hide
That a black and white cow once used.
I ask, "Why was she so abused?"
Over the floor are scattered beans,
Near one wall an empty cage leans.
One room is all covered in oats,
In another I picture goats.
It is cleaner than all the rest;
There is clean straw that is not messed,
A wooden trough ready to fill—
An empty barn just sounds too still.
As I look through a crack I see
some smoke from the nearest chimney.
The sun is beginning to set;
I have not climbed the hayloft yet.
Up there are boards, broken and gray,
And bent-up tin cans, thrown away.
It smells so stale, not like it should,
Outside the air is fresh and good.
I'll breathe deep and then walk away;
Perhaps, come back again some day. . . . .

AT PEACE WITH MYSELF

Dear Lord, let me be at peace with myself,
Then I shall be at peace with everyone else.
No hidden demons will block my view,
Every moment shall be contented, living with you.

Doubts, anger, hate, perplexes will all subside.
Living daily with myself they are taken in stride.
Though inner thoughts seem to be disturbed, too,
Knowing no one can be happy from an outer view.

Peace with myself is really knowing myself,
Not pretending and acting like someone else.
God help me to accept these thrilling interparts,
Knowing they, too, were created perfectly by God.

Peace, in God myself now I can clearly see
All the beauty that surrounds and enchants me.
I see beauty in the simplest, unusual things;
I understand why God planted Himself in the heart of man.

It's so wonderful to be at peace with my own self,
Then I can understand and help somebody else.
God's given love will always find its own true place,
By loving and giving and helping the human race.

ON BIGOTRY

In an age where vice abounds
And bigoted statements are the sounds
That haunt the quiet, hallowed grounds
Of the underprivileged throngs
(Those to whom this age belongs);

In an age where put-downs flow,
Man has no greater foe
Than his tongue. (If he lets it go!)

* * *

ON A QUOTE (By Gordon Merrick)

"If it's love, the Lord won't mind."
A shame that we are years behind
This quote, which is so aptly timed
Yet heeded not. (We can't be kind.)

To love we must first stop hate,
But kindness is only used as bait
To snare the loves that could be great,
And make two-facedness the trait.

Perhaps in time what I love most
Will not be haunted by the ghost
Of hate who comes our way to boast.
When that day comes, I'll raise a toast!

FOR PEACE

give to me a better time,
a stronger truth, a worthy rhyme
a share of hope and unity,
resulting thus in ecstasy.
the world is still for all its stride,
we live illusions of the tide,
and echoes pierce from miles around—
yet not a living, *breathing* sound.

we wait in anguish, awkward fear
a brief deliverance from tears,
a fleeting smile may lift a sorrow
but day revolves—and so, "tomorrow."
from *all* the heavens, souls released
there echos but a single word—"peace."

* * *

LADY JANE

a truer title worthy of
no other gallant slave.
betrayer, nay—a giving soul
so more than others gave.
a grand dame, the beauty proud
of flaxen hair and ashen eyes
oh! lady jane, forever
is the grief of idle time.

125

EVENING BROTHERHOOD

Our neighborhood contains a certain brotherhood:
The men still bend to cut the evergrowing grass;
The gleaming blades look as inviting carpets should;
The rakings cease as fellows stop and time goes past.

The calls of playful children fill the cooling air
As they continue racing up and down the street.
The winner crows with gleeful pride and tangled hair;
The loser smiles through gritted teeth at his defeat.

With gentle love and bliss the resting women stand,
Discussing happenings of hours just barely flown:
Young Jody Brown has built a castle in the sand;
The Widow Jones has welcomed home her son, now grown.

The sun no longer lends its warm illumination;
Too, tiring children vanish from the ev'ning chill.
Soft peace pervades the night—the envy of all nations.

INDIVIDUALITY

The faith that I believe in,
No man's hope could find.
The love that charity brought,
But hate concealed it all behind.

The joy that life left,
The pain that couldn't be put in the past,
A tear is always shed,
But what becomes of a memory that doesn't last?

* * *

LIFE

Fragile, yet brutally used.
Love's journey, hate untold.
Mystery that experiments unfold.
Joyousness that walked with sorrow.

What have I that you do not?
What beckons me and lets you be?
Music with our beats the same,
Clashes and leaves you with fame.

FRIEND

Are you my friend?
   Is your life existence mine?
      You are not my friend.

Are you my friend?
   Will my love and hate be yours?
      You are not my friend.

Are you my friend?
   Would you give me what I ask?
      You are not my friend.

I am your friend.
   My life is not your life.
   I will not love nor hate with you.
   Your asking would be forsaken, if not needed.
Am I not your friend?

We are friends,
   For our compassion for humanity is just.

VICTORY

Just in a thought it may be changed,
Just in a nod it may be improved,
Just in a glance may one take hope,
And surely in a smile will cheerfulness appear.
Don't give up but go on through,
Plowing—sowing—reaping, too.
Never stop even though severe the trials,
Continue on to victory.
Think of Him who daily watches over us;
Ever-present, kind and true.
Trust in His word which never fails,
Be strong—take courage—and go on, son.
In spite of the oppression of the opposing foes,
Plant your feet firmly, put on Christ.
Take up your sword—the Word of the Lord,
Let it strike where the Spirit leads,
And above all, take the mighty shield of Faith,
Look continually to Jesus Christ.
How can you fail? Impossible—for He is victory,
So "Thanks be unto God who always causeth us to triumph,
In Jesus Christ."

A PRAYER FOR OTHERS

Lord help those around me,
Please, Lord, I pray;
In Thine own way let them see,
Thou art the Life, Truth, and Way.

Lord, let not these people perish,
For Thou died for them, too;
Lord, have mercy on each, I beg,
Have mercy, Lord, have mercy.

Lord, if only they knew Thee,
As their Saviour, Lord, and King,
That their soul could be set free,
Then they would shout and sing.

Lord, touch their hearts, I pray;
They know not what they do;
Lord, Lord, Lord, I pray,
Let them realize what Thou can do.

Let not my mouth withhold Thy story,
Which the saints of old have told.
Let me witness for Thy Glory,
Wherever Thou may allow me to be.

SOMETIMES TO TOUCH STONE

Sometimes to touch stone, to smell tar is to see
a strange flower buried
in our distant blood, and so fleeting powerful
to erase the sky of night
and to put a sun there. . .
then we stand among city towers
or in a field of yellowed corn,
and set ourselves on some hill,
more to taste our courage if we have it,
Aware of the many secret changes within
and to remark our cowardice, and we have it,
more than all to see outward and inward
how much sand or granite sheathes us.
We stand by our fellows and breathe their souls
each into ours, into our blood,
a silent brief breathing of agony, hope, love.

We who seem to celebrate death, to wear it as the daily
bouquet of our lives,
festooned about the ritual of war, and yet go on living
practising trivia,
might not wonder why young black men choose to die
shooting it out with the police?
Does this stir us beyond our biers to grasp at a less
carefully kept temperature?
Anger is not enough, not violence, but resolve
to penetreate the tempered steel of our defectiveness, to
shatter it day after day.
The mountainous steel will not disintegrate till we stand
fighting our death.
A taste of exaltation in our mouth, we begin to tracer
ourselves back to danger,
on the taut rim of resolve wink at chaos:
We hold our hands to other men.

GOLDEN SUNSET

Golden sunset on the sea,
Whisper and confide in me,
The secret of those lands unseen
Where mortal men have never been.

Of untold mysteries you can solve
Of places round which you revolve,
Of things all men would like to know
Of time and space for all to grow.

Give us courage to seek the truth
And with your guidance find the proof,
Embrace us in your magic power,
Brighten each one's darkest hour.

Grant us wisdom and peace of mind
The knowledge we ever seek to find,
Free us from the doubts and fears
Which hold us captive through the years.

Mary K. Ebbert

EVENING

Evening steals softly, a shadowy form,
A sweet little lady in gray;
With a faint rustling sound
Her skirts brush the ground,
Sweeping the sunbeams away.

As light as a leaf she descends from the sky,
Blown by cool winds from afar;
With silken caresses
Day's noise she suppresses,
Replacing the sun with a star.

A mystical fairy magician is she
Transforming the earth in her flight;
For the day's scorching ray
Must this siren obey
And melt into shadows of night.

Oh, calm evening stay, gentle spirit, be kind,
With your wand soothe the weary of heart;
Won't you, sweet lady fair,
Free each mortal from care,
Ere you in the shadows depart?

MY SUNSET

The sunset was so very
Beautiful, radiant colors of
Heavenly hue reaching
Across the far-flung horizon.
If I tried to duplicate its
Beauty on canvas, it would
Not embody its heavenly beauty.
But in the scope of my vision
Only I know how lovely it was.

* * *

TO MY BELOVED

I cannot think beyond tomorrow—
Never to see you again!
I cannot fathom the memory of
Places we have been and the
Road of life, often rocky,
Shared for better aftertimes.
Keep within your heart and
Memory just a tiny place;
Let it be mine,
Never to be replaced.

NOW AND ETERNITY

How beautiful the day,
How lovely the night.
How great the mountain's height
And the sea's vast delight.
How lovely to feel the warmth
of sunshine
And the coolness of the waves;
How joyful it would be
After life's tasks are done,
To welcome with happiness
The solace of the tomb.

* * *

NATURE

Nature asks nothing of you;
Enjoy to the utmost
Whatever you see.
Let the loveliness of what you view
In life's endless procession
Rest within your heart and soul.

THE IMMORTAL HUMAN SOUL

God gives mysterious force of life,
    Working in the human temple;
Creates human sanctity, saints
    Striving for eternal glory.

Flaming inspirations of the Holy Spirit,
    With holy sublime ideals inspire.

Cold death, soul leaves for judgment;
    Bodily functions cease.

* * *

THE SEA GULL

Wings outspread, the sea gull flies, soars
    The vast bright blue dome of the skies
Above, silvery, glittering, sunlit waves;
    White, foaming, roaring breakers.

Like a white-winged spirit
    Soaring in joyous rapture
From the earth, high in the blue
    Above the ocean's sandy shore.

THE REBUKE

The planes are fighting in Europe,
Over England and Germany.
They dart and fly—
Great birds of steel dealing death,
Rockets of fire from the sky.

What do you see in that tangled mass
Of wreckage on the grass?
Is he German or Englishman?

God looked down at the fair face
Streaked with blood,
And gave the world the answer:
"He is my Son."

* * *

TO MOTHER

Her hand was gentle as summer wind
That touched and blessed.
Her voice gave comfort, sweet cheer
when needed, and encouragement.
Her eyes were saintly;
Love filled their heavenly blue.
God's wisdom leaped from them;
Thru her—He came alive to you.

Her radiance lighted home,
Priceless her worth and work.
So silently she came and went
One scarcely sensed her presence,
So tiny a footprint
To leave a world of emptiness.

THE ROBIN AND THE CHIPMUNK

Missus Robin looked from her perch,
    And she sort of twitted,
As Mr. Chipmunk came running,
    From the ground he'd slitted.
And Missus Robin said out loud,
    "He thinks I'm half-witted.
I know that he is here to steal,
    My babe that's just been hatched;
I shall out-think that striped rodent,
    Before my birdling's snatched.
He'll soon find out—that ol' ground squirrel—
    That he has been outmatched!"
Mr. Chipmunk was brave and bold,
    He sat so still and staid;
His mind was working out the plans
    Of his great escapade.
And Missus Robin shook her head,
    And felt a bit dismayed.
Mr. Chipmunk could almost taste,
    The succ'lent robin meat;
To himself he said, "At last I
    Shall have a robin treat!
I'll take that bird—mm-mm—piece by piece—
    And that no one can beat!"
Then Missus Robin flew next door
    To talk to Yellow Cat;
"If you'd like *pièce de résistance*
    I'll show you where it's at.
That is of course—if you don't feel
    Too, too, aristocrat!"
"Of course, I'll come! A cat's a cat!
    And besides, nowadays—
Its best to 'strike when the iron's hot'—
    To quote a paraphrase.
How can I know how good it is,

If I don't first appraise?"
Yellow Cat slunk under the fence,
   No time for tête-à-tête;
One quick glance at Mr. Chipmunk,
   No questions! No debate!
Yellow Cat ran with lightning speed,
   But Chipmunk didn't wait.
He ran across the yard posthaste,
   The cat was on his tail;
Then he ran across the gully
   To better hide his trail.
Though Yellow Cat was speeding fast
   'Twas all to no avail.
Mr. Chipmunk just disappeared,
   Yellow Cat was cheeky—
Because he snatched a passing mouse,
   That was sounding squeaky.
And Yellow Cat thought it quite right,
   To be a little sneaky.
He took his booty home. A mouse
   Whose tail dragged on the ground;
He didn't care a penny's worth,
   That it was on rebound.
"Besides," he said then to himself,
   "He's fatter and more sound."
Missus Robin was overjoyed,
   Everything was ship-shape;
She tucked her birdling in at last,
   And enjoyed the landscape.
"My, that was fast," she said out loud,
   "No mess and no red tape!"
Chipmunk was a bit unraveled,
   He felt somewhat uptight;
He could hear Missus Robin singing,
   Besides—he'd had a fright.
It seems that only he was sad,
   But then—it served him right!

IF I SHOULD DIE

If I should die some night
    While you slept peacefully;
I say if I should die,
    Shed no sad tears for me.
I'd slumber on and never wake,
    Although you'd cry and tear your hair,
and even if your heart would break—
    I would not care.

I would not hear you tell,
    The things I loved to say;
Your thoughts wouldn't mean a thing,
    After I turned to clay.
I would not know if you had cried,
    I would not hear you heave and sigh,
Yet, when you hear that I have died,
    Don't ask, "How did she die?"

If I should die some night,
    I would not care for sympathy;
I mean, if I should die,
    Bring no bouquets for me.
I would not see the grand array;
    The grief of my repented foe,
For like a piece of moulded clay—
    I would not know.

And when you clasp my bier,
    And sadly shake your head,
Your kindly words will fall
    Unheeded when I'm dead.
I want to feel your friendliness,
    I need a helping hand RIGHT NOW—
I say, waste not your kind caress
    Upon my icy brow!

140

THE HOUSE OF YOUTH

She wandered lonely down the road,
That for many years she had known;
Stopped at a house: 'twas Youth's abode,
In a garden with hollyhocks grown.
She softly knocked on Youth's white door,
"Who knocks?" he melodiously cried.
"One whose body is old and sore,
And seeks Youth once more," she replied.

"'Tis sad," said he, "You cannot stay,
The sands of time I cannot waste;
For those who leave my door one day
Can't turn back! But travel on in haste!"
She knocked again with a weary sigh,
The house shook with a clamorous din;
Youth's voice rang with an angry cry,
"'TIS LOCKED! I CANNOT LET YOU IN!"

* * *

A THREAT

That squirrel that comes each day to feed,
On food that I set out for birds;
Who stuffs his chops with bread and seed—
Is going to get much more than words!

THE MASTER ARTIST

God, how dost Thou paint all the sky so bright,
Before dusk falls upon the silent night?
The crimson Thou hath painted 'cross the skies
Hath brought sweet joy to my admiring eyes.
Thy rich, deep red, mauve and purple, too,
Are skillfully blended, resting 'gainst Thy blue.
Thy red fades into salmon, orange and rose,
And lights Thy western sky like candle glows.
All streaked with deep blue-green and dusky grey—
They softly tell Thy world. "Gone is the day!"

Thy loving earth and sky's embraces meet,
Wrapped in Thy deepest blue and purple sheet;
And fading fast, Thy crimson-red turns pale,
And dying 'neath the grey they tell Thy tale,
Then one by one each star appears on high,
As the dark, silent night doth reach the sky.
Thy MASTERPIECE, each day, is ever grand—
But even I, Oh God, can understand.
And love Thee more with all my humble heart—
Because—greatest of all artists—GOD, THOU ART!

I'M LISTENING

I heard the wind across my back,
I felt it whiz and sharply crack;
It carried leaves—like running feet—
My neighbor's barrels down the street.
The hiss and roar inside my ears,
Intensified my awe and fears
With smarting eyes and burning tears.
There was no doubt within my mind,
A wind so strong was not designed
By any man. No man could claim
To spawn such winds; or even tame
a gale that leaves men powerless;
Sweeps through men's hearts with raucousness,
And where it goes no one can guess.

A rain that beats down mercilessly,
And pounds with great voracity,
That brings a noisy, thundering quake
And leaves one helpless in its wake.
The flash of lightning across the skies,
Makes even strong men agonize—
Small-minded men to rhetorize.

How can we doubt Your presence here?
Though many have been known to veer;
No man could hang a star on high;
Fix the moon and sun up in the sky;
Some even say that You are dead!
And truly, some have been misled—
I'm listening, God, to YOU instead!
I'm listening, God, to YOU instead!

WHEN PA GITS HURT

My Pa he hurt his hand one day while fixin'
    the pantry door,
He screamed like he wuz gettin' kilt an' flung
    his hammer on the floor.
An' Ma bathed Pa's hand in water—t'wert the best
    that she could do,
She painted it with iodine cuz it turned red,
    an' black an' blue.
Pa, he'd walk aroun' the house an' he would sort o'
    grunt an' sigh,
He kicked all the chairs aroun' the room an' he
    poked me in the eye.
All us kids got awful scairt when Pa commenced
    to wail and roar;
He moaned an' groaned an' oh boy! How he cussed
    that danged ol' pantry door!
Now lissun, folks, Pa hurt his hand an' he sure
    wuz good 'n sore.
Now he got waited on hand an' foot, so I hope 'at
    you will see—
How menfolks act when they gits hurt an' the
    critters that they be!
Now—my Ma wuz cookin' dinner an' the stove wuz
    burnin' hot,
She reached her hand to turn the key an' laid it
    on the coffee pot.
Ma drew her hand with a little gasp an' painfully
    closed her fist,
Us kids, we all runned, an' saw a burn from the elbow
    to the wrist!
An' Ma—she kinda smiled an' sez, "Here, you kids,
    now go an' play,
It's jus' a little burn," she sez, "an' purty soon
    t'will go away."

Pa sez that Ma wuz careless an' she shoulda had
              better sense,
An' not ta reach across a stove. An' b'george!
              he went an' put a fence
Aroun' the stove, so when it gits raily red
              an' burnin' hot,
She can't reach across an' rest her arm on a
              boilin' coffee pot!
But Ma she jes' kep' right on workin' an' n'en she'd
              kinda sigh,
I looked at Ma an' n'en I knowed, I see a teardrop
              in her eye.
When I seed the blister on Ma's arm, b'gosh, it
              made me cry.
Now—I ain't complainin' 'bout the men but I hope 'at
              you will see—
How wimminfolks act when they gits hurt, an' what
              wimmin raily be!

IT'S OVER NOW

It was yesterday we smiled together,
Our thoughts were always true,
And now I want to clear the past
Of memories of you.
Something sudden changed our ways,
We were no longer true;
All our thoughts were twisted and worn—
Life to us seemed forever torn—
You and I will never be,
Our world is far apart.
Whatever happened to a beautiful love?
I know not where to start.
T'is no use trying to make amends
For I cannot forgive your sins,
If ever I chance to cross your path
Don't touch me—for I am cold at last.

* * *

THIS LIFE OF MINE

My life is just like an ocean breeze,
Its natural air and all;
And yet my life is no different
Than the firmest concrete wall.

My life is full of glory,
Just like in early morn;
Although its trials are often,
My heart is never torn.

MARTIN LUTHER KING JR.—
AND THE BLACK MAN'S WAR

Martin Luther—the black man's priest—
Stood on the boardwalk for a poor man's peace.
Martin Luther Thy vision did feast,
Cried in a loud voice for a dying man's lease.

Martin Luther—the author of love—
Held to the banner of an earth-moving dove.
Martin Luther—a knowledgeable man—
Stood on the balcony with a righteous hand.

Martin Luther—a conqueror of change—
Threw in the lifeline with the widest of range.
Martin Luther—a God-given man—
Was called to the altar to take his stand.

Martin Luther—though heaven his home—
Lives in a black man wherever he is known
Martin Luther and the black man's war,
Changed an America—this Martin saw.

PEKINGESE

The mini dog of China
Sits on a cushion of red velvet;
Long, thick hair of oleo tan
Encloses the quiet little face.
Fragile, refined, and polished
As a freshly cut ceramic.

Hate not the little dog of China,
Ye who whistle for a comrade
To chase your stick in the park,
And lie at your feet in the evening
To show his strong gratitude.

Behind those understanding eyes
Are dreams of a forgotten period
In a great antique age of culture;
Memories of pride, dignity, and valor,
The practice of good manners.

The mini dog of China,
Once the companion of king and queen
Today he is but a trinket
Sitting on a red velvet cushion. . .
O man and woman of high degree
Remember the antique practice—
Learn from the little dog of China.

BEAUTIFUL COLOR THE WIND

Beautiful color the wind
When whirling past the mill,
Gold is the color it sends
Through sleepy daffodils.

Beautiful color the wind,
Green when playing on hilltop,
Deep azure among bluebells,
White with forget-me-nots,
And smoke grey in the dell.

Beautiful color the wind,
When refreshed by April showers
In the early morning hours,
A conglomeration of colors
In a garden full of flowers.

Beautiful color the wind,
Pressing wide trails of purple,
Softly over evergeen trees
As lilies are whitely encircled,
Brown the wind over fallen leaves.

* * *

ATLANTIC CITY, N. J.

We sat in the moonlight on the beach,
Between the sea and the land.
The whole sky seemed in our reach
When we sat there on the beach.

Wave sounds fell softly in our speech,
The wind played with us hand in hand,
As we sat in the moonlight on the beach
Between the sea and the land.

WE'RE HERE, AMERICA!

"Give me your tired, your poor,
Your huddled masses, yearning to breathe free,
The wretched refuse of your teeming shore,
Send these, the homeless, tempest-tossed, to me,
I lift my lamp beside the golden shore."

America's present Negro Immigrant Generation,
Yearning to breathe free after 300 years of
American oppression; this star-crossed,
Half-starved flotsam and jetsam of a long-wrecked
Planter Society, homeless in America after 300 years;
This Negro, damned by skin color to be an alien after 300
Years of American residence, this is the late
20th-Century American Immigrant Generation. Never citizen,
Never settled, never at home, never accepted,
After 300 years of violated rights, pride, opportunity,
hope.

"I lift my lamp beside the shining sea."
No, this generation of immigrants aren't coming
From "over there," across thousands of miles of ocean.
This generation of 20th Century American Immigrants are
native-born.
They have simply never been admitted to citizenship.
They have never shared American wealth. They have
Never shared American hope, opportunity, freedom.
They have just been here. And we, and our forebears,
And theirs, have not admitted it. We have not
Admitted they were here, and citizens, and have not
admitted
Them to any of the rights of citizens. Now they come

Knocking at the cities' doors and saying "We are here.
We are here. Here in America. Here in America with our
papers,
First-class citizenship papers. Try to bar us. Try to
Deport us. Try to deny us. We are here. We
Were always in America. Before the wars. Before the peace.
Before the freedom. Often, before you and yours.
But this is different. Now that we have endured slavery,
And the slave-breaker, and the man-breaker; now
That we have endured the Klan, and lynchers, and a
Hundred years of denial of our Constitutional rights;
Now that we have endured hunger and deprivation, and our
Klan terror
And Jim Crow obloquy; now that we have
Endured the ghastly non-humanness of your city ghettos,
And the realization that the White Man is Christian when it
Pays him, or it doesn't hurt him, or somebody puts it
across on him,
Now, we are here. You can no more prevent it than we can.
For
This is a Day of Reckoning, America. Nobody will put us
Aside and forget us for another hundred years. Nobody will
leave us to
Our Fate. Nobody will act as though we blend into the night,
As though, because we're hungry and cold and voiceless and
Powerless, we aren't here.

"Because we're *here*. The new Immigrant Generation. We
migrated
Once, like cattle in slave-ship holds and we were here. We
were once given
Full constitutional rights, a hundred years ago, on paper
and again we
Were here. But this is our Immigrant Generation. We've
moved on again—
Out of hunger and terror and degradation in the Southern fields,

151

Where we were dispossessed croppers because we never shared
in America's
Land-holding privileges. Uneducated and untrained, because
we never
Shared in America's social rights. Hungry and deprived, because
We never shared in our country's economic opportunities.
Stateless—they thought—since the law saw fit to
Define the Negro as inferior, and the custom was to deny him ev
Right and opportunity. But, starved and dispossessed, we moved
But still within America, within our native land. And we
are here,
America, the Mid-Twentieth Century Immigrant Generation.
Reckon with us.

"Other immigrant generations, you let through the
Gates at Ellis Island. We're in. We'll show you our papers.
Others you let into the ghetto of slums and poverty and misery.
'Fight for your rights,' you said, and they did. And we
will, too.
But you admired them if they fought, and you let them move
up to
High Street. But you look at our papers, and our skin, and
You say, 'You're Negro. It's the ghetto for you. Permanently.'
But you're fooled.
Now we know our rights because some of us learned to read.
The earlier
Immigrant—his son got a good job. But you look at us and
say, 'You're
Negro. We can't let you amount to something, because for
Three hundred years you've been here and we've denied you
everything—
The common rights of man, constitutional rights. If

We didn't go on treating you the same way, it would mean we've
Been wrong for three hundred years. Go back to the ghetto.'
But we have news.
We've learned our Constitutional rights, and we've learned
That the Supreme Court are suckers for justice, and we'll
HAVE THE LAW ON YOU. We're here America. Our Immigrant
Generation, yearning to breathe free. And we know the Supreme
Court's OURS, too.
We're here, 'masses, tempest-tossed,' ghetto-housed, hungry,
Under-educated, but we're here, America, expecting to
Participate in American Democracy FOR THE FIRST TIME.
FOR THE FIRST TIME. FOR THE FIRST TIME. In American life,
FOR THE FIRST TIME. To dream the American Dream, too, FOR
THE FIRST TIME. For we've stayed Outside longer than any
Other immigrant group, in quarantine for 300 years. But now,
WE'RE HERE, AMERICA. MAKE WAY!"

SPACE AGE
IN A LATTER-TWENTIETH-CENTURY OFFICE (B.C.)

We watch Hour Zero on the color screen, as astronauts
return from Space,
Witness a small exhibit of the heroism of the race—
While down the office corridor Boss watches—us.
There is a file to file, a "t" to cross, a thing to do,
Urgent, punctilious, timely, critical, methodical, payable.
So, bound to earth, we are reminded of Man in Space.
So, lost in space, we are reminded of man earthbound,
Eyeless in wormhole, matching earth to earth. We
Are errant; we should be doing the correspondence or
At least, as a gesture, cleaning out a file.

Splashdown! And still some men travel their familiar
Earthways, officeways, antways, rooted to
Treadmills of the mundane and the familiar, fearful, even by prox
To soar. A mere child's imagining has through the ages spanned
Space on Pegasus. Today—when as adult, man has finally
Matched the soaring imagination of mere child—at the mere
childhood
Of the race—there is an Alter Ego who,
Distrustful of all but stark Reality,
Escapes as camouflaged machine amidst machines,
Captive of Drudgery, worker ant, a mole habitual.

CHOICES

Cherry bloom in fountain falls,
Daffodils on window sills,
Forsythia leaning over walls,
Color from each corner spills—
All the world's alive.

Old men nodding over letters;
Writing memos to top brass;
Girls transcribing for their betters,
Waiting for the day to pass;
All the world's a tomb.

When the spring's out there, to claim,
When new life's to catch and hold,
Why share self-destruction's blame?
Why share four walls with the old?
All the world's a choice.

Beauty's free, and duty costs all,
Joy of life is sun and air;
Why be office drone who's lost all,
When Sweet Nature's young and fair?
All of life's for living.

When a day of heaped-up beauty,
When a day of reckless fun
Measures aeons for the duty-
Ridden, busy civ'lized one,
Let's be pagan zanies!

Life and beauty, Nature's dower,
To their shrine let's homage bring;
Without walls and bosses dour
Every man could be a king;
Life's a song we're meant to sing.

Every shoot and sprout is festal,
Every flower's the world's rebirth:
Leave behind the dull, the banal,
Tend the blossoming of earth;
Life was made to celebrate.

* * *

TRIBUTE TO SPRING, WITH IRS

Green grow the rashes, oh,
Greener the tribute
To Uncle's coffers flowing,
Your wealth to redistribute.

Spring, youth, the world renewed
We hope to win;
IRS turns any joy—e'en Spring—
To "living in sin."

"Where did you get that?
How did you spend it?"
Whatever you thought was yours,
Uncle but lent it.

Beauty and flowers aglow,
Spring season hail.
Uncle is dunning YOU and YOU
By every mail.

Life springs anew and seems
Yours, yes for aye.
Computers work your tax
To take you on the sly.

Green grow the rashes, oh;
While IRS watches;
Think not e'en Spring is yours
If UNCLE catches.

156

ELEGY WRITTEN ON AN OFFICE TYPEWRITER

Let us tell in mournful numbers
Of the soul that's dead or slumbers
Till a lifetime's work is done
And Retiree turns to greet the setting sun.

What dullard, in what school begat,
Lives nine to five, and turns his head to fat
That he in his retirement class may claim
He gave his All to labor and to fame?

He never learned to live, nor play, nor sin;
He never learned to love, nor hate, nor win.
He never learned to be, nor feel, nor try.
Only Job existed 'twixt *his* Earth and Sky.

Keep his Job-worshiping cult away
So I may love my life, both night and day;
So I may thank God for life and liberty
And not be yoked with Ass to Job mortality.

Let him learn life—if he can—in a Retirement class,
It takes more than credits and a few hours passed.
People must learn this art of Living day by day,
Or they might miss the Show if they should Pass Away.

Or, did they first? The funeral hour's not set,
For any of the men and women whom I've met;
Some choose their own, in Life's despite,
Walking a corpse that clanks his chains by night.

NEVER SAY NEVER

N. .ever say never, think it over once or twice,
   then once again, yes, why not make it thrice?
      It is better not to decide in haste,
        time is precious and should not be put to waste.

E. .very day there are problems too numerous to mention,
   plus all the other things that claim one's attention.
      It has often been said: "I hope I'll never have
      another day like this,"
      but while still in the land of the living days
      like this one can't miss.

V. .ery often mistakes are made to which we vowed
      "never again," and there's no explanation;
   at times like these we are led to feelings of frustration.
      When minds are quickly changed and plans turned
      to naught,
      we need a little more patience and forethought.

E. .ver hear of the woman who, when asked to marry said,
      "Never!"
   Of course we've heard, but she thought she was being clever.
      But love conquered all, when proposed to once again
      after he asked not once, not twice, but a total of ten.

R. .ight we may be, but wrong we stand corrected;
   it all depends how our lives are affected.
      But the things about which we say—"NEVER"—to
      are the very ones that we so often do. Isn't it true?

SMILE

S. .mile, even though your heart is breaking;
   only God knows the effort you are making.

M. .any people you will meet along the way;
   telling them your woes will not make you gay.

I. .n this world filled with care and sorrow
   keep smiling, for there is always a tomorrow.

L. .earn to be patient and bear in mind,
   by your smile another friend you'll find.

E. .ndless are the days when you're feeling blue
   but a smile costs nothing, 'twill see you through.

MARCH 10TH

It was the night the City, so silently creative
And bedecked in its finest jewels,
Put on a show. There from the top
Of a nearby mountain the people
With the same dream opened their eyes.
The invitation had no words—the host
Merely sent a feeling. Then began the
Revealing of its gigantic treasure of beauty.

While the crisp winds of night sent Sounds
Of Promise through the swaying branches
Of trees so eager to sing, the City blossomed
Into an endless array of multicolored splendor.
The people gasped when they saw their
Dream, shimmering with excitement,
Reach up and embrace all things around it.
Paralyzed they stood.

MY RETIRING SPEECH

Many a time have I thought of this day, and events would run
through my mind.
Taking stock of the years I spent at 156, and the aftermath I
leave behind.
Time is such a gripping force, within its forceps tight,
It takes a week, a month, a year, and crushes them with its
might.
And so the many years have gone by taking its toll in many
ways,
But it brought me friends and family, with blessings that fill my
days.
For a special thing I am grateful and thankful to the powers
that be,
That all through my teaching years, my sisters were here with
me.
Like an ever-glowing sunbeam from a radiant sky
Were the moments we spent together, even if only in passing by.
In the lunchroom or at a conference, wherever we chanced to
meet,
It was a gladness of heart and a most delightful treat.
Like the fossils on bedrock imprinted for millions of years,
So deep in my heart are the imprints left by you, my special
dears.
When days were tough and weary and burdens fell my way,
There was my constant heart companion, my Harry who
brightened my day.
My children were my inspiration; in my classroom I was kind,
I loved everyone's children, because my children were in my
mind.
Teaching was my calling, for children were precious to me,
Each day meant a new challenge how good a teacher I could be.
Each child meant to me a mother's heart entrusted to my care;
To betray that sacred trust I couldn't and wouldn't dare.
I came to school quite prepared for into my classroom I
brought

Love and cheer and patience, with fondest good wishes
wrought.
Now how can I say "farewell" to you, my dear and loving
friends?
With most of my life spent in your midst such friendship never
ends.
I'll recall your smiling faces in the stillness of the night,

And your charming chitter-chatter with affection and delight.
I'll recall the bits of gossip that we whispered to each other
And the love that went with it from each one unto the other.
All of you I fondly embrace now, with a heart filled to the
brim,
May the years ahead bring you joy; may that feeling ne'er grow
dim.
I want to thank you for every kindness, please forgive any
transgressions of mine.

To err, dear friends, is only human, but forgiveness is divine.
Some people look at life through a mirror; in a mirror your own
reflection you can only see.
I tried to look at life through plate glass windows, so that I
could perceive humanity.
So I hope my career was successful from the beginning unto the
end,
For I brought light to little children, and in each of you I leave
a friend.

TO MY SON, WHO GRADUATED FROM MEDICAL COLLEGE

Make your goal a lofty purpose, in every word and every deed.
Service to your fellow man, a listening ear to the human need.
Let your eyes be ever watchful where you can be of service best,
And your ears for calls be listening, and your tongue with kindness blessed.
Let your head be ever thinking with your heart as a constant guide,
And in parades of glory you'll be marching with the greatest, side by side.
Put a price upon your labor; let compensation be "work well done."

Great men feel contented when their fellowman's respect they've won.
Let your lips be tinted with kindness; in your ways you must instill
Hope and trust and even friendship; prescriptions write with a humane quill.
Like an artist on his canvas we make our imprints on the sands of time.
Do your work in such a manner as will reflect an image that's noble and fine.
And your deeds will be recorded in the Greatest Book of All,
In the depths of your own conscience, in the hearts of those who call.

JIGSAW PUZZLE

Life is a jigsaw puzzle,
        pieces scattered here and there;
although some are of bright hues
        there are dark ones everywhere.

Latest puzzles now are round
        where once all of them were square;
so much of life is a circle
        and the game is not played fair.

This only goes to show us
        that in our puzzle of life,
each piece must fit a pattern
        that includes both joy and strife.

If, when the trial is greatest
        and our faith is at low ebb,
we'll only trust the Savior,
        He can keep us from a web.

The pieces we have broken
        in our zeal to place them right,
by Jesus can be mended,
        puzzle-perfect in His sight.

THROUGH THE EYES OF A CHILD

Are clouds really made of cotton
    white—floating through azure blue?
Is there real gold in the sunbeams
    to be caught and bagged by you?

Are all flowers made of velvet
    just to please the human eye?
Are cobwebs on the dewy grass
    placed as traps for you and I?

Are rainbows spun of silken threads,
    ends tied to a million spools?
Do songbirds sing to all alike?
    Are mermaids in limpid pools?

Does Cupid fly when there's a moon
    with his quiver and his bow?
Does stardust sprinkle to the ground
    making diamonds in the snow?

Who is to say where magic lies,
    where bewitched and where beguiled?
The simplest things bring pleasure
    when seen through the eyes of a child!

LITTLE GIRL ME

I look at me
and see
many ages,
but mostly little girl.
Little girl in search of life and loving;
Little girl who sometimes fears the dark;
Little girl who needs strong arms around her;
Little girl who seeks her treasured mark.

No one yet has kept a promise made her,
No one yet thinks life is only she.
No one yet fulfills those needs that age her,
No one shows the caring constantly.

At times I must regress,
I guess,
but only
to identify my needs.

I am no butterfly;
a metamorphosis will not occur.
I am no different
now from then
or ever.
I am so much a woman
in need
not to be alone,
the little girl inside me
cries out loud.

D. T. Fresolo

GROWING

Trees grow straight,
  their skyward branches reaching with arms open wide.
They hold life;
Trees grow side by side.

Vines crawl along the earth,
  clinging to everything, seeking places to lie.
They choke life;
The vines will die.

Trees grow straight.
  They grow singly side by side.
And yet——
  Their branches touch,
    their arms entwine.

D. T. Fresolo

ALONG THE BEACH

The ocean was still as glass today
      as I walked along its shore.

The same ocean that holds you;
The same ocean that makes the distance between us grow.

I caught some water in the palm of my hand.

And I held you.

* * *

THE BRIDGE

To bridge the gap of generations
      the old must bend—
      the young must reach.

MYSTICAL ROSE

At the forking of the roads—I saw you there—
One leading to the orchard knoll,
Facaded by the rows of fruited white figs,
Only vagrant refugee of Eden's lush untilled.
Below gold-weighted muscats drowsed
Beside a rank-edged water ditch half-filled.
The other wound through flower gardens,
Blazing red and gold and green in sun and shade.
And in the "Y" in hidden bower
A lute and harp strained out their plantive plea
In life's nostalgic airs.
And wondered I it all conceivably should be.

At the forking of the roads—I saw you there—
A sheaf of roses in your arms.
I knelt to bend an opening bloom
And saw new worlds within its lovely folds
Where men with souls might live
In love and peace, and strive toward more eternal goals.
I heard the strains of martial music
Trilling out from peak to cliff through air pine-scented,
Sharp, to sting the soul to vivid life.
And disenchanted by the glow and glint of gold and gem,
Here will I kneel and live a thousand years. . .
Until the New Jerusalem.

* * *

HYPOTHESIS

The birth of love
Is known whereof
Exists the kiss,

As similies
Are poetry's
Hypothesis.

MAGIC MOMENTS

Lift the magic curtain of the past
where are recorded the highlites of each day.
What it was like to be young and aspiring
in an era so inspiring. . . . .
When music disarmed the mind,
thoughts ensured musical expressions
and winged its way to new dimensions. . . . .
Capturing the general aura—the joy of living
that embraced the tranquility—the flavor of life;
the key was involvement in those magic moments.
Life tinged with opportunities
time did not erase the memories. . . . .

* * *

AFFIRMATION OF A REALTY

Visible was the absolute clarity of the light—
from the sunset and the stars so bright,
from the sunrise shining on the massive majesty
              of the snowcapped mountains,
the rain mists that crowned the wooded hills,
the fresh clearness of the different greens
              in the valley,
the symphonic strain on a rolling hillside. . . .
              In the rush beyond the roar
              I inhaled deeply the fragrance,
              A serenity of the hour—
              It was there my spirit guided me. . .
              The love of travel left me within
              A power of a well-planned continuity.

NEW LIFE

The daffodils are in bloom in my garden today;
How wonderful if always they could with us stay—
With their new green coats and golden crowns,
Seem to be spreading the glory of God around.

But no, they can only for a short while stay,
Then slowly and silently fade away
And disappear into the earth—
And again next year shall have new birth.

So like us humans, who at life's end
Go to sleep for a while—
But we too shall be born again.
The Lord is showing up, thru these lovely flowers,
If we trust in Him—
New life shall be ours.

THE PENNY GOES TO CHURCH

A big silver dollar and a little red cent
Rolling along together went.
Rolling along the smooth sidewalk,
When the dollar remarked—
(For a dollar can talk!)—
"You poor little cent,
You cheap little mite,
I am bigger and more than twice as bright—
I am worth more than you a hundredfold,
And written on me in letters of bold
Is a motto drawn, a pious creed—
'In God we trust' for all who read."

"Yes, I know," said the cent—
"I am a cheap little mite,
And I know I'm not big
Nor good, nor bright—
And yet," said the cent
With a mean little sigh—
"You don't go to church
As often as I!"

LONELY POODLE

There is a lonely poodle in town tonight—
They took him away, though he put up a fight.
He looked in my eyes, as if to say,
Please, oh, please don't send me away.
I'll be good if you let me stay—
I won't bark at those squirrels though they
Shake their tails at me—
Yes, I'll try to be good as a little poodle
can be.

Dear little poodle, they won't let you stay
At the hospital here, for even a day.
So be a good little poodle and stay at
the vet for me—
And I'll try hard to get well, and come get you
As soon as can be.

JEALOUSY

Jealousy goes by another name;
   Green-eyed monster, his tongue
      a flame;
Once you are under his wicked spell
   You know the agonies and depth of hell.

He wrecks your body and warps your mind;
   Wherever you look it's evil you find,
For you see all through his evil eye—
   You'll wish you were dead—and fear
      to die.

Once he is in complete control
   All is lost, may God rest your soul.
And love? Oh, love dies a horrible
      death,
   Withered and burned by the monster's
   breath.

* * *

NEVER ALONE

When morning comes God takes my hand
   To guide me through the day;
Though I may stumble now and then
   I shall not lose my way.

And when the evening shadows fall
   I still shall have no fear;
For I believe with all my heart
   That God is always near.

174

HOME

Tall and stately does it stand
    at the head of the street.
White stucco with Colonial lines,
    a wee mite weatherbeat.

Ivy climbs upon the porch,
    and up the steps and rail.
Many winters has it weathered
    winds that did prevail.

Hedges run around the house,
    all trimmed up and lean.
Washed, every now and then
    by rains to make them clean.

Shady trees surround the place,
    where birds in spring build nests.
Squirrels climb the walnut trees,
    seeking nuts with zest.

A garden hides behind the house,
    all tucked within a wall.
Many hours are spent out there
    in the spring and fall.

A bird bath stands down in the yard,
    where birds and squirrels reason
It affords them an oasis,
    during summer's long dry season.

The swing hangs down from the gnarled tree,
    with its seat still swinging.
Remembering children so gay with mirth,
    and high-pitched voices singing.

Inside you'll find quite comforting,
    with colors blended through.
Every room throughout the house
    all filled, but nothing new.

Old pieces lend themselves
    to each room with decor,
Standing high on cupboards
    from ceiling to the floor.

Wyeth prints line a stairway,
    each speaks of real deep living.
God, and nature, color, and grasses,
    and humanity, forgiving.

Old bureaus and chests fill upstairs rooms
    with woods that shine in glory.
Would that they could but speak,
    and tell to all their story.

Patchwork quilts upon the beds
    once worked by loving hands,
Now show to all, with stiches small,
    gay patterns, o'er life's span.

"Pennsylvania Dutch" is blended
    here and there.
"German Spatter" lines a ledge,
    once molded with great care.

Fruit jars stand in windows
    all filled with different beans,
The "blue-grass" kind that are so rare,
    stored once in barrels unseen.

Antique lamps that now shine out,
    once filled with oil and flames,
While little children played on floors
    as lights flickered over games.

Rocking chairs that rocked the young
    are found in many rooms,
Where mothers sang their songs of love,
    dispelling fear and gloom.

The church that stands just down the street
    peals out the evening chimes,
Calling out, to one and all,
    pray to your God Divine.

Look around you, every day,
    and count your blessings, do.
What you do, and how you do,
    is truly up to you.

Riches are in what you do
    for family and neighbors.
Your thoughtfulness in how you do,
    in giving love and labor.

These things all make up my home,
    reflect my daily living.
Live for others, not for self,
    and be forever giving.

BUILDING WITH GOD

Lord, help me as a Christian man,
Help me to build as Thou dost plan,
Thou art the Superintendent here,
The Master Builder, Overseer.
Help me to choose the very best
Materials that pass the test—
Combine faith, hope, and charity,
With honor, zeal, sincerity.
The foundation Thou dost provide,
Thy Holy Word our rule and guide,
And if good work we have in mind,
Then we must follow Thy design.
And when the contract here is done,
Full payment Thou wilt give each one,
With promise that as each has tried,
His talents shall be multiplied.

* * *

PRAYER

I'm grateful to Thee, Lord, for prayer,
To know when I pray Thou art there,
Art never too busy to hear,
But to me Thou wilt lend an ear.
Forgive me, Lord, should I complain,
It's nothing compared to the pain
That Thou didst undergo for me
While on the cross at Calvary.
Help me to do that which is right
And ever-pleasing in Thy sight,
So when my life on earth is through
In heaven I may begin anew.

178

AT THE COURTHOUSE

When for the jury you are called,
It may not be so bad,
You just serve three weeks, that is all,
And a good time may be had,
For if you are not on a case,
All you must do is show your face.
They have TV and some magazines,
There's a coffee break in between.
While some folks pass the time away
By playing cards, women crochet,
Or perhaps some of them recite
What they intend to do tonight.
Of course, they'll let you out to eat,
By three-thirty your day's complete.
While some decide another's fate,
They also serve who sit and wait.

A PICTURE WINDOW IN THE COUNTRY

The autumn sky this morn is gray—
There's a crispness in the air.
The trees are colored, oh! so gay
As their autumn clothes they wear.
We have a picture-window view
Of earth, and trees, and sky—
A view so picturesque, yet real
As birds go winging by.
A picture window's worth its weight
In gold throughout the year,
By bringing every season's beauty
Through panes so bright and clear.
As nature does her very best
At what we know as Fall,
Through glass this golden flame is brought
As a picture on our wall.
In daytime we are apt to see
A plane across the sky,
While the moon in all its majesty
At night goes drifting by.
We watch the children at their play
And wind, and rain, and snow—
A road of gravel to the house
And people come and go.
It seems there's plenty to be seen
Through panes so bright and clear—
A sense of joy and peace it brings
To us throughout the year.

SPIRIT LYNX

The lynx stood on the lonely hill,
The totem of the tribe,
And wailed into the evening still
His frozen cry inscribed:

With loneliness and just a tear
For cohorts now long gone.
Where is the tribe of yesteryear?
Who occupies their throne?

The lynx's eyes as starlight shone,
His tufted ears turned out.
He pondered where the tribe had gone
As they were not about.

He saw his tribe had made a change
As the seasons make their rounds.
They'd drifted to a further range—
The happy hunting grounds.

And yet he wailed unto the hills
'Til it echoed in clefts and chinks,
'Til all who heard shuddered with chills
At the sound of the "Great Spirit Lynx."

DAY BREAKS BUT SLOWLY

Tread softly upon my dreams. . .
Do not awaken the winds of Yesterday.
Let me gaze the sky in its face
And look with joy to the dawn of morning.
For you kept vigil with me during the Twilight Years—
You caressed my fevered brow and brushed away my fears.
Yet many were the moments I longed for you,
And thought you no longer dwelt with me but in my thoughts.
But you were always there. . .
I in my pain could not glimpse you through the Darkness,
Yet I felt your warmth as it searched my sighing heart
And pierced me with the sweetness of your love,
Smoothed the wrinkles of my soul—
Restored to me the faith in life—
Gave my spirit a time for rejoicing.

* * *

ETHEREAL

The stars rest merrily on their blanket of blue,
Giving light to the Wisdom beyond.
Man on the outward horizon,
Yields to the silent glow—
Inspired by the vastness of the Eternity about him.

THE BEGGAR

He has no houses and land;
    He is not a wealthy man
Who has achieved fortune and fame;
    Nobody knows his name.
To his hovel he goes like a mole
    That crawls to his tunnel hole.
Dirty, ragged, and gritty,
    His state is certainly pity;
Just another burden for society,
    And a case study for piety.
But have you stopped to pause
    And wonder about the cause?
What manner of man,
    Always with empty hand?
His wit may be scarce and dim
    Yet God has made him,
Tho beggar, ragged and old,
    The keeper of a human soul.

THE MAN WITH EGG ON HIS FACE

In utter obscurity he languishes,
Though thoughts of heroic proclivity
              obliterate
A mundane existence. . . .
With unfounded doggedness and zeal
He flounders in pretentious persistence.
His menial tasks befit his needs,
Completely unresourceful;
He looks at you with crusted eyes,
Spaniel-like and remorseful;
Yet dreaming of his other self,
In some daring exploit or place;
In a crowded train he gapes at you,
The Man With Egg On His Face!

* * *

TIME

How fond the fingers of time must be
Of youth, its strength and gaiety;
Yet in its kindness disdain abides,
Concealed by beauty
A mask of ugliness hides,
Unbeknown its fingers mold;
a withered face,
parched and old;
How cruel the fingers of time must be
The aged to sculpt unheedingly!

THE LONELY CHERRY TREE

I know a forest deep and dark
which never heard the song of a lark,
nor did it see the lovely May
so lost it was, so far away.

There in a narrow hidden place
a cherry tree bloomed with a snow-white face.
Just like the moon, so lonely and bright,
it stood in the forest's ancient night.

The seasons came, the seasons went,
the tree its bud and blossom spent.
Entrapped by the forest's silent loom
in the world it knew no other bloom.

There came one spring to this lonely place
a silvery owl with a magnetic gaze
and told the tree of magic leas
with a thousand blossoming cherry trees.

"Like harps they sing, like fountains they rise,
like a legion of angels in disguise."
The tree heard the voice as in a daze
it shook its roots, it tore its lace.

That night, enwrapped in silence and fog,
the lonely tree suddenly started to walk,
it walked through the forest, down to the leas
and joined its brother cherry trees.

FOOLISH CONVERSATION

Three fellows met
one lovely day,
a squirrel, a lark and a pretty jay.

Said the lark:
I look so dull, so dusty grey
I wish I were brilliant blue like the jay.

Then the pretty bluejay complained:
Oh that I could spiral as well as a lark
would crow to high heaven from dawn until dark.

The squirrel giggled:
Strange fellows you two,
I am glad I resemble neither of you.

I don't care to dip
my head in a cloud
would rather have supper than song in my snout

and I do very well
without a blue vest,
for jolly jolly me, I like myself best.

* * *

DANDELIONS

Summer meadows dewdrop cold
in their dandelion gold
dandelions fluff and suns
whirling wheels in dazzling dance
now in demonstrations run
because the gardeners will have none,
proclaiming to all: take heed take heed
dandelions are no weed!

186

MUCH TIME HAS PASSED. . .

Much time has passed much time
since magic May came to my door
with fragrance, bud and fire core
and on a farflung magnetic behest
the silvery song returned to the nest.

Much time has passed much time
since hopes flew high
like kites in the sky
and radiant life had nourished my soul
first tender, then thunder, then humbly and whole.

Much time has passed much time. . .

                    *   *   *

WHEN TO NAKED BRANCHES. . .

When to naked branches icy wrappings cling
in the deep of winter
buds perpetuate the spring.

Clad in armour, hoods and pelts
they slumber under bleak and snowswept skies
until the fist of winter melts.

While nature in its frozen cradle sleeps
the waking mind can sense or see
the thread and flowing circle of eternity.

THE FIRST CHRISTMAS

The Christ was born for all the world,
Not just for you and me;
For all the sons of Abraham
Of whatever creed they be.

There are those who embrace Islam;
Also numerous Jewish clans;
All are, indeed of Abraham,
Though they inhabit many lands.

Christ was born for those who live
Afar beyond the widest sea;
How wonderful to know that this
Includes all life that thrives
As well as you and me.

Even helpless, deprived babies,
Only saved for Science's cause;
Those who have that spark of genius
And can claim the earth's applause.

Let all the clever ones of earth
Now keep the sacred laws,
And remember man of woman born,
May harbor human flaws.

The virtue of Eternity was born
On that ancient Christmas time,
And the human laws that govern men
Took birth in every clime.

CHILDREN OF NATURE

Bird music is natural and free;
The warbles we hear from a tree
Ere the sun rises high
To light up the sky,
Are the songs that delight you and me.

The eagle that floats in the sky,
That soars with the clouds up on high,
Thinks not fondly of earth
Though it gave him his birth,
He savors the freedom to fly.

The robin that hops on the lawn,
Seeking tidbits from earliest dawn,
Is not working for us
With our praises and fuss,
But for fledgings so soon to be gone.

The nightingale sings for himself;
He sings not for power or pelf;
That the mob hears his air
He is too proud to care,
He warbles to God and himself.

The whip-poor-will sings near a stream;
His pensive notes blend with your dream.
When the day goes to rest,
His vespers are best,
His laments are for God, it would seem.

REQUIEM OF THE ELMS

The lovely elms that gave us shade
Are felled and hauled away;
The music from their boughs is stilled
All is silence and decay;
The friendly birds and saucy squirrels,
Homeless, have gone away.

Folks were warned if treated early,
They could save the pleasant trees,
But no one heard the warning
Of this ill, borne on the breeze.
Thoughtless folk just moved on,
Unmindful of all pleas.

Sidewalks upon our streets are bare,
No birds or squirrels to sing or chatter;
Now where will robins go to nest?
I think is a quite serious matter.

Now sadly we go forth each day,
Upon the naked street,
Hearing not the whispering branches,
Or the birds in their retreat.

Why is man so deaf to warnings?
Or the maxims of the wise?
So tardily we weep and mourn
In silent, sad surprise.

OCTOBER REVERIE OR BIRTHDAY THOUGHTS

I walk upon a mottled street
All strewn with colored rain,
Of Autumn leaves blown by the wind
And heaped from lane to lane.
Vexation of spirit I do not find—
I find profit under the sun.
When winter comes I'll not fear it
Nor its fierce rigors shun.

All summer walked I in the sun,
That long daylight hours spread,
I quite forgot that fall must come
When summer warmth had fled!
But Autumn came on colored wings,
Though Autumn days are fair,
We know that soon wild winds will blow,
White snowflakes fill the air.

Shall I be sad to weep and wail,
For Summer days misspent?
I hope with bold and forward step,
I'll plod the snowbound trail!
No lifetime lasts forever within this earthly bourne,
Know respite from life's toils and pain,
Not you, but friends should mourn.

DID YOU EVER?

Did you ever walk between
Raindrops on a cool spring dawn?
Ever slip beside one and catch
A few diamonds in your hair?
Have you ever swung on a morning glory vine
And come to rest on a shiny green leaf?
Ever touch the flowers reverently
And feel their velvety softness?
And then slide down to rest
On the cool carpet of grass?
Did you ever hear a pine sing
Its soothing song only to you?
Have you ever nestled between the petals
Of a big red rose and taken a snooze?
Ever go swimming in a drop of dew
And then climb upon a honeysuckle vine
And drink of its refreshing nectar?
Well. . .did you ever?

TIME

As I grow older each passing day
I often wonder what fortunes will come my way.

I have lived in an age of sophistication,
Cutting corners and modification,
When imitation substituted for authentication.
It has been the age of instigators and advocators,
Agitators and calculators.

There is instant food and the instant printer,
Instamatic cameras and for sport skiing—instant winter;
Deep freezers and home air condition
Hi-fi sets and color television;
Backyard barbecues and swimming pools
And mini dresses and boots became the rule.

This world has advanced at a fantastic rate
Since Adam and Eve did officiate.
I only hope that peace will rule the world instead of war,
For if the world is destroyed,
The difficulty of starting from the beginning once more
Is a fact we definitely cannot ignore.

DON'T JUMP TO CONCLUSIONS

No one can look at another man
And know what he has on his mind;
No one can create another man's plan
Or know what fortunes he might find.

When you criticize and compare to others
Or tear down and degrade one another,
You might not know what burdens the other man bears,
Or how overwhelming might be his cares.

A man may not tell you all his woes—
And of all his stories nobody knows. . .

If a man does not choose the path that you follow
It might be that he is a little taller,

And if he does not want what you have to sell
Perhaps he is creative and can do just as well.

So to jump to quick conclusions
About someone else's plight,
Is spiteful, indictful, and just isn't right.

A TINY RED BIRD

Come, little red bird, please come to me.
Come closer, so that I may see.
You don't speak my language, that is true,
But please let me communicate with you;
There is no one around, but just we two.
Your beauty and song I very much admire,
For without you and your bright attire
The whole, wide world would soon go wrong.
God, our Creator, made you, it's true,
Rest assured He had a purpose for you.
You add beauty, song and hue
To the beautiful skies so blue
As from tree to tree you go flying through.
It's nice to pause and hop about
And give me a chance to observe you on your route.
Stay, little red bird, and give me a chance,
I want much, much more than a glance.
I'd like to tell you and reassure you, too,
Before our conversation is through.
You've inspired me—without even a word
Although you are just a tiny red bird.
Now it's my time to daily life return,
I really want to show more concern.
Maybe I can with others share
Moments like ours—so precious and so rare.

Connie M. Haun

NOT A WORD!

Listen! Listen! It must be a bird!
It's the sweetest music I've ever heard;
Don't interfere or try to disturb.
They are telling us without a word
About the beauties of their baby birds.
Listen! Listen!
Isn't it the best sermon you've ever heard?

* * *

SPRING

Red, yellow, blue and white—
The flowers are blooming with all their might.
The grass is green and growing tall;
We'll have to cut it until late fall.
Birds are singing here and there,
It's so easy to tell
That spring is in the air.

Connie M. Haun

BREEZES

Have you ever watched the breezes?
They whirl up and they whirl around.
Sometimes they are sideways,
Sometimes they are down,
Not always gentle and slow;
It's the motion which pleases
And keeps one at ease.
At times I've wished that I could be
Just like the breezes,
Not to be found anywhere around.
Come now, little breezes—make me free.
I want to see and feel how
It is to whirl and twirl away from the town,
Go miles and miles and not be found.
"Thank you, little breezes—can't you see
Lots of people want to be free
And go about their duties with more ease?"
Even, at times, do just as they please?

CAN YOU SAY, "I DO?"

Do you take this woman
To be your lawfully wedded wife,
To do as she pleases
The rest of your life?

To serve her coffee in bed
When she sleeps late?
To speak of constant love
In spite of occasional hate?

Do you solemly promise to wash her clothes
And everything else, only heaven knows?
Last but not least, will you always be true?
But before you answer, the words are "I do."

* * *

POWER

We've come into power,
So they say. . .
The heads of states
Have paved the way.

We've died—we've struggled
We've pleaded and foregone,
But in the end—
Have we won?

Let's get united,
And stand the test,
When real power comes
We'll be more
Than the best.

SILVER HAIR

Tic-toc, Tic-toc
Back and forth, back and forth,
  It was the sound of a clock;
It created such a strange melody
  Each second and day by day it continued.
You sat in a rocking chair,
  It was next to the window,
A breeze from outside the window
  blew the waves of your silver hair.
Were you buried in meditation again?
  Were you meditating on your fast affection?
Or were you thinking about that
  unforgettable enmity and deep hatred?
Otherwise you might have to bear in mind
  an unfinished dream.
Oh! Life has colorful pages,
  but it also has some chapters of darkness!
I was close to you and used
  my warm hands to rub your cheeks,
Oh! How the tears—like cold water—made your face wet!
  What memorable moments caused you to become emotional?
Every recollection usually makes people grieve.
  Why don't you look for the silver hair of brightness?
Of those shining colors you should be proud;
  They show your unlimited experience in life!

THE BEACON SHINES

A beacon is a glowing signal
That shines and glitters as if to peal;
And with a sound that's like a squeal
I know its purpose is to appeal.

It's heard and seen, though I'm not sure,
For I still dread its bright allure.
Some sailors do find it safe and secure—
Landlubbers beware, for it's no cure!

They count it as faith, hope and wonder,
And trust it as they would a brother.
Their faith, hope and wonder is like a tower,
Not unlike the beacon they stop to ponder.

It's heard and seen, though far from shore,
The Beacon Shines forevermore.
It tells me of ships that came before,
And how the rocks emerged and tore.

The Beacon Shines to me a warning:
The rocks beneath are quickly coming.
And yet I know from her loud ringing,
Home lies beyond the rocks now threatening!

IN W'S EYES

I love the private smile your eyes do hold—
The smile that seems to gush from caves within
Your heart to eyes that make it grow until
It is a loud, but soundless, laugh I see.

Although at times when I'm alone and think
Of how your smile can grow until it laughs
I wonder—would it be, that you're amused
At such as my naive simplicity?

This doubt goes on and grows, until I'm sure
The caves within your heart are ringing with
The laughter spent in poking fun at me,
Believing there is privacy in smiles.

The scruples age, and go where scruples go
When next we meet alone, because
I love the private smile your eyes do hold;
It's not so hard forgetting doubts I had.

PUPPET SHOW

"Crook one
Finger; Please
Pull the string."
          A puppet
          Impertinent!
"Please, Lord,
Pull the string,
Make me happy soon."
          How selfish
          To bother Him!
"I weep;
Everyone
Else has fun."
          Poor puppet,
          So sorry
          For just itself!
"Please, Lord,
Pull the string,
Make me happy soon."
          Poor puppet—
          He cannot see
          Anyone but me.

Emeline Henderson

DEAR ONE

Dear one,
While you are young
Mark things down
Now and then
Your perplexities and frustrations,
Leave out none;
Your restless tears or gentlest joys,
Mark them well.
In some far day in time to come
You will look back, and
Reading and remembering,
See your own
Dear one.

LIFE IS A GIFT

Life is a gift a purpose and love,
And by the preeminence of the above.
Yet adversity reigns in a changeable reign,
With nothing the same, yet many hearts sing.
For often we're glad and sometimes sad.
Mysteries unfold much to behold,
While ages past and ages come,
There's a first and a last for each and every one.
In this world of ours there's much we say,
About poverty, fame, but there's a brighter day,
And it's not in gold or silver we pay.
A mystery unfolds that will never decay.
Then eternity shall reign and darkness shall go away,
And we'll ever be free from a world of dismay.

WITHIN THIS WORLD NOT OUR OWN

All through the ages mankind has roamed,
His journey within this world not his own.
Many scenes past are already gone,
Stake memories that last, as they're shown.
But earthly substances will forever soon end,
And that of greedy hearts of created sin.
And by the twinkle of an eye, there will then,
Be eternal glory of no end.

* * *

PEACE IS AN ACCOMPLISHMENT

Peace is an accomplishment
Of each individual, group or body,
That of one's own and each individual goal,
The fruit of thine own hand that brings rejoicing to the
soul.
A workmanship in true reality in a peaceful harmony with
others.
Magnified in love by the fruit thereof,
That lighteth the way of good will unto all men,
That the tiniest life live to its fullest capacity.

TO THE MUSES

Hasten, Muse, let us go
From gay delight to saddest woe.
Usher in thy favored child,
Born of Gods with human wiles,
Stalwart, proud, with humble heart,
Possessing, demanding our love from the start.
Forever he holds in his small right hand
The newest song, God in any land!
Arouse, Child Poet, touch our hearts,
Give us a song we long to hear,
A song of man, of earth, of sky;
"Follow your fancy," we long to cry,
Or laugh or dance if that be your will,
The magic lyre has too long been still.
"A song, a song!" The whole world cries
To the poet for a song that satisfies:
  A song to break the stillness,
  A song to greet the bold,
  A song to fill with gladness
  Hearts sorrowful and cold;
  A song to sooth the weary,
  A lazy, languid lay
  That will banish all our heartache,
  And only the Muses play.
  Bring us verses of simple sweetness,
  Mingle our joy and grief;
  Show us the pain of beauty,
  Of love and passions brief.

AN AMERICAN AT THE COMMUNIST WALL

Hello, Comrade, together let's laugh, chortle and chuckle!
(Hide carefully your conquests so painfully gained.)
Where is the honor in walls that encircle
A people who cluster at holes to escape?
Talk to me, Comrade! Stay at my window
So open and friendly as free men receive
All those who fly here, dig, race or die here,
Creep from beneath your tanks that enslave!
Hi, Comrade, ol' buddy! Are you
Suspicious of Yankees with all of their play?
You're a boot-stomper, table-pounder,
A master of intrigue, thriving on greed!
Vodka drinker, peace-talker, blockader, gatekeeper,
Betrayer of people you crush with your creed!
Church-wrecker, soul-smasher,
Saluter with cannon of nations you bleed!
So long, Comrade! Are you proud of your power?
Feel secure and content wherever you stray?
Sword-rattler, gloat while you may for a judgment awaits you—
A judgment awaits from the ghosts of your deeds.

* * *

MOMMY, WHAT IS GOD?

God is
        An artist, a singer, a laborer, a cook,
        A mother, a teacher, a writer of books;
        The faith of Man aged, dying in pain,
        Certain that sunshine follows the rain.

ON NEWS OF THE DEATH OF A LOVED ONE

Happy little tick-tock, busy all the day,
Where does time come from, where does it go,
As you diligently tick away?
Where is the time for living?
Where is the time for play?
Where is the time for seeing
Loved ones at home or away?
O cheerful little tick-tock,
Each second passing by brings another swiftly
As the hours hurry by, and the days and weeks and months
And the years add up as well.
Was it a century in passing, or only a tick-tock-tick-tock,
tick-tock?

* * *

BIRDS IN THE BAMBOO

Birds in the bamboo, why do you come?
Safety in numbers, hidden at night,
Then rustling, chirping, a swish—and you're gone
Just at the point when dark turns to light.
How can you dart so sure from your cover?
Who is your leader, your unfailing guide?
How do you know where the bamboo offers
A safe place at twilight for the bevy to hide?
O tall bamboo of the feathery branches,
Some call you a monster with roots so untamed.
As you nod and beckon those aerial playmates,
Please warn that Tabby is doing the same.

ANGEL UNAWARE

Man's inhumanity she knew,
War's whistle, whir, and shriek;
Too young for bitterness and hate,
Wan waif, immobile, meek.

In tattered skirt and toeless shoe
She waited wordless there,
Not knowing that soft halo haze
Lay light on matted hair.

On field-cut feet she came a step,
Dry wistful eyes looked up—
So gaunt, the pinched and hollow cheek,
Such want, an empty cup!

Compassion for His own He felt;
The Christ willed comfort, care
While we, so blind, did entertain
An angel unaware.

* * *

TEAR

O eye, keep back your migrant mist,
Becloud my vision not.
Often has that request been mine
When anguish was my lot;
And then I found the tear a lens
Of God's great telescope
That brought within my narrow view
The essence of live hope.

EVENING'S GIFT

We walk together in dusk's vibrant hues;
Gentle breeze from warmer lands
Encircles our hands and delights inside us.
Her head is bowed as she, too, reaches for golden bits
And pieces of what perhaps is a secret long locked
In an ancient vaulted crypt, a neolithic thought lost,
A fleeting promise, or a future dream.

And what would become of the stars, if we
Could grow into timeless giants and reach
For those fiery, sparkling rewards, gather them,
Collect them into our open hands, turn and
Fling them, streaming through the night,
Until they stopped in new places, hanging from
Different strings in the cloudless heavens?

Would they not be as beautiful?

For stark against a black image, lit be the moon in fullness,
Great stands the pyramid, each crack gazing back,
As we are not the only storytellers.
Were our wisdom fancy or calloused grown
The night would close quickly, shadows passing free,
A gentle breeze from lonely lands, reflected in a myriad sea.

Lyman Gilman Hill

FAIR HELEN

Fair Helen Campbell:
One summer day
I once dreamed that thee
Would be sitting
Across the table breakfasting with me
O'er eggs and bacon,
Discussing the merits
Of Samuel Johnson and Euripides:
And later at dinner,
Sitting across the rosewood table,
Speculating on happiness to be
In the garden of the Hesperides,
Where red apples
Hung heavily down from red astrakhan trees;
And Europa splashed on Zeus' back
On her wedding flight
Across the blue Aegean Sea
To the Minoan shore;
Where you and I,
Under the blue Mediterranean sky,
Would sing of heroes and study Greek philosophy
And gaze upon the shipping on the blue Minoan Sea.
But now, since these things were not to be,
I now hear the owl in the winter apple tree
Announcing the coming of the cold
In my garden,
Where that summer was pure fancy.
And now my memories are gold,
And the ships that would have delighted you and me
Have long since gone from the blue Minoan Sea.

THE WOMEN

We are weary of the war drums, we are weary of the strife.
We are women, mothers; He was God who gave us life,
Life to pass on to another, life in sacrifice and pain.
We are through with war and famine; we are our true selves
again;
We are links to God, Creation. Never again our sons are
riven
From us; never again wailing, weeping women, hungry, starving
for life given.
We are reasoning, thinking women who give and give and give.
From "The Day" we are refusing to give life that cannot live.
There are older men in reason than the boys that we have
brought
To an earthland that shall harvest all the beauty of their
thought—
All the beauty of their building, all the magic of their
dreams.
At their mother's knees they're listening: "Life is what it
seems;
Now in infancy, now in beauty, now in relationship to God,
A brighter age is growing out of the old subconscious sod.
That nations must fight endlessly to conquer fear of other
men,
Of other men, their brothers, for the Age of Light is here,
when
You shall know no death in youthtime, no disillusion, Dear,
For the age of war is passing, the Millenium is here.
You must learn your lessons early, you must learn to think
and build
To a better age God promised, right here to be fulfilled.

Herb Hofmann

IN THE SOUL OF MAN

As long as there is hate in the souls
    Of man, it's hard for man to understand.
Why should they fight for just a cause
    Because they want to believe the
Right from the wrong? Don't they
    Know it's a sin to take a life?
Maybe little children and also a wife?

God did not create man and woman
    To be slaughtered by human beings.
It's time for men to mend their ways
    And be careful of whatever they say.
Life is so short, so why
    Not make the best of it while
You're here on this earth?
    What American means to me
It's not like American used to be.

RENDEZVOUS

Terrible with light they came
to that terrestrial rendezvous,
set by celestial plan long eons past. . .
converging on a microscopic point
of earth. .leaving the vast universe behind. .
with joy unspeakable they sang. .
Shining Ones from that far place
of mystery and God. . .

The thunder of their glory struck
a dark and silent field in Bethlehem,
and shepherds lifted trembling hands to God. .
then simply this. . .an angel spoke. . .
this was the time to be come true;
one need not perish now. .the Lord had come
to an infinitesimal speck of earth
from a far off Blessed Country. . .
He had arrived to die. . .

* * *

EVIDENCES

He must be God, as He said. .
only God would come seeking
a straw manger. . .a bloody cross. .
and the perverse souls of men.

214

MOTHER

Mild-mannered you were, canny, wise
To all the cunning child deceits
And faults, but quick to sympathize;
To understand those sudden heats
Of passion bursting forth in tears
And rage, yet curbing with a hand
That soothed and quieted our fears.
Our mundane world you made a land
Of dreamlike beauty, oft a-throng
With little folk or souls divine;
And all our hearts you filled with song
And music, gentle mother mine.

* * *

MONEY'S WORTH

I thought I'd made a fair exchange
Today—my dollars spent for strange
Gay frills by which I was beguiled,
Until my eyes beheld the child:

A child, wide-eyed there in the rain,
With snub nose flattened to the pane,
Quite unaware the rain was there,
Her dreams bright as a solitaire.

So, as a child, I too would stand,
A few small coins clutched in my hand,
All windows scanned, my eager eye
Could vision what those coins would buy.

Of all I bought today, there's naught
Returns me half those small coins brought,
When I exchanged a few centimes
For wisp-like threads of childhood dreams.

WHAT CAN HE KNOW?

What can he know? What can he know,
This little one whose fingers go
Like dancing elves, trippingly,
From branch to branch of the Yule tree?

Delighting in its prickly sting,
Its pungent smell, the tinkling ring
Of tiny bells, he smiles and cries,
"It's beautiful!" While in his eyes. . .

(To me the tree is rainbow-bright,
Alive with scintillating light,
And fragile tinselled mobiles that
Are made for eyes to wonder at!)

What can his thought of beauty be—
This child who has no eyes to see?
What can he know? He speaks anew,
"It's beautiful! Christmas is, too!"

He needs no shiny tinselled strand
For in his lightly straying hand
He's captured much the finer part—
The Christmas glow within the heart!

BLACK GANGS

Help!!! Help!! Help!
Blackness is felt—Colorwise,
Destructivewise and Otherwise.

Travel with me and not alone,
In a community that is not your own,
Riding or walking, looking right and left,
From behind there might be theft.

Educated Black Men of strong will
Educate Black Gangs not to fill
The Black Community with destruction,
And wrongdoing construction.

Plan ahead for a better day;
Black man, White man, Green or Hay;
Place the world with *good* cooperation;
And make the heavens above accept our operation.

* * *

FORMATION

I have been to the mountaintop of hope,
Assured a Promised Land for my folk;
"We Shall Overcome". . . . .I hope;
All of the Negro-blooded folk.

Reverend Martin Luther King
Lived to bring
The importance of things;
Black folks brings to ring,
To the country and nation,
For lifely better formation.

217

SCHOOL IS GETTING OUT—OUT OF HAND

It was 8:15 and as a general rule
I was entering for another day of school.
Coming from the mailbox I spied the clock on my right,
Today I promised myself I wasn't going to get uptight.
I ascended the stairs in time to hear one girl remark
about the night she had,
And in the company of the boy's father, whom she thought was
just as bad.
She talked of the food and liquor she consumed—
I thought of these remarks as I hurried to my room.
Then at 8:30 come the faces of despair,
Children walking aimlessly, it's plain they don't care;
Now it's first period and a student is asked his intent,
And he replies, "You must think that you're some M.F. prince."
Needless to say this created uproarous laughter
The young teacher sends to the office for assistance in the
matter.
It's now lunchtime and the kids are at their lockers,
They are yelling, screaming, and kicking them (lockers) for
shockers.
I walk over and ask, "Is this necessary?"
As so often they now play the role of the adversary.
A few angry words are exchanged with much ado,
Then they leave and say that they're through.
Finally the bell is ringing, a student replies "School is
out!"
But in the hall, a teacher and a student are exchanging
shouts.
I then go out to lend some assistance
And find some students think it's none of my business.
They then purge their souls of all abuse—
I warn that acting like this is no excuse.
I ask them to leave or face suspension;
One remarks that he has no intention.

In my room I start a summarization,
He stands and smiles with utter degradation.
Now he yells "That's all you can do is write,
But you know what we can do—settle it with a fight!"
He says a few more things beyond belief
And when he finally leaves it's a relief.
From this I hope you can understand
Why I say school is getting out—out of hand.

MAN IS A CONTRADICTION

Never satisfied with what he's got—
Always wanting what is not—
He's forever seeking, it seems,
Chasing after his elusive dreams.
Holding to thoughts concerning where,
Dreading to be here, longing to be there;
Seeking and searching for things ever new,
Happiness in finding it, sorrow sometimes, too.

When he's young he wants to be old;
More privileges he'll have he's been told.
But reaching old age, there's the sad truth
Of his yearning for the days of his youth.
The boy who is thin and wants to gain weight
In middle age has a change of heart when it comes too late.
Those who are short want to be tall,
And tall wish they wouldn't be noticed at all.

Women with large breasts who wish for small,
Are balanced by women who want to have all.
Hair color changes from day to day—
Brown, black, or was it charcoal grey?
Blacks using bleaching creams on the 7-day plan;
Whites flocking to their sunlamps for a glorious tan;
Plastic surgeons work at a feverish rate
Just trying to keep pace with the changing state.

A man without is called poor;
He wants to be rich and nothing more,
And those who possess the wealth and the fame
Say that they may not be all that people claim.
There are men who are in who want out
And that their places would be filled is without a doubt.
That man is not satisfied there can be no doubt,
And if he can, he'll change what he's got.

LIFE CAN BE BEAUTIFUL

Life can be so beautiful. . .
If you listen with your heart and mind
For the true love you seek
You will surely find.

You must have hope and courage
And look forward for happiness,
So listen to your lonely heart
To find warmth and tenderness.

Listen while your heart speaks
And you will learn to grow,
To live, and to love—
When love enters you will know.

As you build your rainbow of dreams
Life can be so beautiful,
With the wisdom to understand
And your dreams you will fulfill.

Listen while two hearts meet,
Softly your love will entwine
So listen with your heart and mind
The faith you will combine.

Your hearts will beat as one
With joy and love so kind,
And the promises to always be true
Because you listened—with your heart and mind.

BEAUTY

Beauty is the stillness
of a moonlit night,
The glory of a quiet dawn,
Perfume of a rose,
Gentle wind sighing
through the leaves of a tree;
Beauty is knowing
there is One
Who made possible
All loveliness to be,
Above, beneath, around us,
He is there—with you and me.

* * *

THANKSGIVING POEM

I have loved you
since time began,
And long after
this great span is o'er,
I shall love you more.
Beauty lies in the
Sweetness of the love we give;
A noble life I have lived
　　　　to know,
And through it I have
　　　　learned to grow.
I joyfully bless the day
I lived to share
The gift of love we know.

THE LOVELY ANNE

The lovely Anne
so proud and fair,
Gentle as moonlight,
Beauty was there.
Proud to the world,
Humble to God,
justice and mercy
flavoured her words.
Flowers of all seasons
graced all her ways;
Perfumed and sweetened
all of her days.
To all who knew her
She was so rare,
She was my mother—
The lovely Anne fair.

REFLECTIONS

Autumn again has come on time
With her gown of furious fashion,
And I, my love, have traveled far
For the brillance of thy compassion.

Thou art as a tender leaf
Humbled beneath the heavens,
Soaring gently in the fervent breeze,
Suddenly waiting as the earth would rain.

Thine hair is like the sundried grass
Mussed with strips of bark,
And in thine eyes such splendor,
Indeed, thou art a treasure rare.

My soul, my life I'd gladly give
To have thee always near,
Embodied by thy warm embrace,
In thee forevermore.

Would thou take thee a worldly chap,
To keep as days may number?
My soul, my life I'd gladly give
To be lost in thee forevermore.

THE CREDO

I am the sum not only of men's shouting
(Though wars and government have ruled my life),
For I have looked on lilacs in white bloom
And savored russet's winey thrill in fall;
I have heard children singing at their play
And felt the friendly warmth of leathern books.
Such things have power and scope to outlive life,
I know. Long after blood is dry, and kingly
Names are sour on men's tongues, the
Dead scent of lilacs still will dust the air,
And children's laughter echo through the years.
These little wonders form the joy of life,
And I shall keep my faith until death comes,
Knowing that somewhere leathern books are read,
Knowing that somewhere russet apples grow.

* * *

THE NEW ENGLAND FARMER'S
SONNET TO BEAUTY

These city folks, they come to me and say,
"From your back porch you have a splendid view
Of forests still and deep, of mountains blue;
I'll buy this farm from you this very day."
And when I answer "No" they go away
To say among themselves, "He never knew
Of night's sky sown with stars, so bright and true,
Of autumn's patchwork quilt in colors gay."
And yet I know of beauty they can't spy:
A turnip clad in lavender and white,
The silver of a kitchen's frosted pane,
The virgin loveliness of dawn's pale sky,
The scent of new-mown hay on a summer night
Why, a farmer sees a world in a drop of rain!

225

SCOTLAND COUNTY WINTER

Winter blows colder
in the South,
where wicker chairs rock on vacant verandahs.
Wrought-iron fences dam
husky leaves, restless,
sibilant with death.
Winds chase each other through empty blue skies,
unbroken by roll of hills;
Black children shiver in white folks' gardens,
they prune and rake for chilly nickels.

All the bright girls
in their red and white dresses,
if they bloom today,
bloom in other gardens.

Southern Poetry
Review/Spring/1971

THE QUILT

Aunt Edith's patchwork:
Hallum history.
Scrap of Uncle Benny's jeans:
He made white lightning and traveled
by freight.
Red satin from Sally's party dress:
Pretty Sally, early a mother but never
a husband to prove it.
White silk from Grandma's
wedding train:
In the center, an old striped tie of Jethro
Hallum's; he founded our fortunes
with Hallum's Seed at South and Vine.
They say he played a gentle harmonica.
I like to think he fell asleep to the tune
of dreams,
A man needs visions.

North Carolina Folklore
Vol. XX, No. 2, May 1972

SUPER SORT OF WIND

The wind that waves the widest tree
　　　　Is a super sort of cart,
So strong and long. . .and never wrong
　　　　In terms of counterpart.
If love were carried by its gust
　　　　Into all smallest part,
The world would gain, creation know
　　　　That love is really art.
Yet if the wind would blow at me
　　　　And force me to the ground,
I'd have to fight it back, as right
　　　　And make it turn around.
No force has right to knock me down,
　　　　To hold me at the low,
I aim for fair and will get there—
　　　　This fact the wind will know!
One day will man devise a plan
　　　　So great and full of right
That fury shall push forth its sail
　　　　Across creation bright.
The imbeciles shall be of past
　　　　No prospect left for them—
Full force for God, for Good, and Man. . .
　　　　The gem from human stem.

WAIKIKI BEACH BY TWILIGHT

When dusk descends on ever-crowded Waikiki,
The happy-splashy sounds of the beach crowd
slowly fade away,
As they leave the surf and swaying palm trees
Until another sunny weekend day.

Homeward-bound cars congest Kalakaua Street
While a sunburnt surfer and bikinied lass
stroll, hand in hand,
As they head for the nearby hamburger stand,
where they can buy a very tasty treat.

The beach is now a dark and gloomy shroud
As the golden-hued sun disappears behind the
distant clouds,
And the only sounds to be heard are those of
the surf and wind,
Recalling what a happy day it had been!

A PLEA

You have left me helpless, a crippled heart,
    adrift on a sea whose utter darkness has,
In these short hours since our separation,
    penetrated the very recesses of my soul.

So it cries out in anguish, slowly sinking
    beneath the waves of love that have often,
Very often, comforted this muddled mind
    and left in its depths ecstatic joy.

I have tried to divine since that moment
    the nature surrounding this love of ours,
And can see only a oneness, a parallel
    of want, of need, of endless dreams fulfilled.

I see your likeness in all things beautiful;
    your voice is the angel choir of a loving God;
Your touch is velvet on a skin of alabaster,
    and your kiss is the breath of life itself.

But I, in my stupidity, have rejected—
    aye, and scorned—your complete surrender;
And now there is naught left for me
    but in humility, to plead thy forgiveness.

Margaret Ricaud Kelly

KINDERGARTEN ANN

She's just fine,
So young and alive.
She goes to kindergarten
And sits on the bench
When she talks and giggles,
Also when she wiggles.
You'd love Kindergarten Ann.
She's so gentle, and
When I ran
To play hide and seek,
To find me
It seemed to take her a week.
Kindergarten Ann lives next door,
And was made to adore.
Her dog is named Frisky.
Kindergarten Ann came one day to tell me
He had broken his joint in the knee.
When she cries I comfort her
Until the tears turn into a purr.
Kindergarten Ann is so wee,
She's a little friend to me.

SCARECROW

While riding by a field the other day
I chanced to see a scarecrow on the way.
His hat was battered and torn,
his pants looked very well-worn;
even his shirt was faded,
and his views looked jaded,
but suddenly he came alive,
with some real mean jive.
It sounded like this and
it sounded like that;
he gave me a dance
and how he did prance;
he kicked his feet,
he looked real neat.
That certain scarecrow made me a bow
the other day, as I passed his way.

Margaret Ricaud Kelly

LIFE IS TOO SHORT

Life is too short for me,
so many things I want to see;
Time is passing too fast,
so many friends have passed;
There isn't enough time left for me.
People say twenty years in school and
forty years to work is the rule,
then comes retirement and what then?
I want to write and I take up the pen.
Life is too short for all of us;
now nothing is worth too much fuss.
A philosopher says man changes every seven years;
count your seven years without the tears.
So many things left to do, say, and see,
so little time is left for you and me;
there are others like us.
We have yet to mold into dust;
we all rush because we must.

PRACTICAL IMMORTALITY

If people lived before this life
T'would seem to me, in times of strife
That they would look ahead of there
Into the future, taking care
That what they now decide today
Decides that future in a way
Not heretofore examined.

If people really lived before
As fact and not a myth, does war
Solve anything?
The babies come, the dead they go
And governments say so and so,
Please watch it, guys, before you whack
The enemy—you may be back
In thirty years or so to live beneath
The very future you now make.

* * *

ON DIANETICS

When thinking thoughts I used to think,
I had to think and think to think that thought.
Leastways that is what I thought I ought.
Have you never so been taught?

But now I find it's really easy;
Think a thought and not feel queasy.
The reason why just has to be
The thinker of those thoughts is me.

SPRING AGAIN!

You must enjoy it, dear;
It's only once a year!

That fragrance that is bound
To dampness in the ground!

That soft and warming rain
Came finally again.

This air feels fresh and light—
The skies are blue and bright;

The creeks are running free
And buds are on the tree;

The birds awake to sing—
From branch to branch they swing.

There is a winter fly
That happily zooms by!

The coming grass, bright green,
Can here and there be seen. . .

Forget now all distress
In early warm caress!

TAX TIME

We all do hate the Time of Tax;
When fig'ring it you can't relax

The highest 'rithmetic no help
But for a specialist you yelp!

The time for Tax is chosen well
As soon you hear the Easter Bell

You can enjoy the greening lawn,
The flowers and a lusty fawn

And with the happy birds you sing
As after Tax there comes a Spring!

* * *

PEACE

Let's welcome peace as it is here
And bury hatred, grief and tear,

But certain ones can't feel secure
That Peace will finally endure. . .

But let's enjoy it to its best
In happiness and friendly rest

'though sorrowful I heard it never
That most good things can last forever—

236

THAT BILL

He was not cardiac before
But lately was near Peter's door

He got the heart machine and pills
And shots and diet—all the frills

And then he was released as cured—
But he could never back be lured

And soon it came—his Hospital Bill—
He dropped and was forever still. . .

* * *

FINALLY A SPRING

Bye, bye, you wint'ry night!
The Sun turns warm and bright;
The snow can't longer stay
It has to melt away—

You can already tell
That buds begin to swell;
You feel it in the air
And birds arrive in pairs.

O, come from ev'ry corner
That we together sing,
As after ev'ry winter
Must come another spring.

HOLD ME

Why did you leave so suddenly at night,
Without a farewell word or hint of a goodbye?
When I tuck my small son in and see,
Asleep, he holds his hand just as you used to do,
I cry.
Or on the street I see a form like yours,
And when the phone rings I hope. . .
Even though I buried you,
That you are not really dead!

A whole year has passed. . .
It's useless to watch for you;
Now I must accept the truth.
It is the longest we have been apart
Since I was born.

I miss your voice, your smell, your step;
You've left me so much to remind me.
My sons, my thoughts, my life itself—
Do you know it and watch when I am unaware,
Then are you near?

If I could only know that you knew my love,
That you were glad of it and at peace—
I'd forgive you if you'd gone
To finally join my mother.

A PRAYER TO MOTHER

Mother dear, where are you?
Far above the sky so blue—
There amidst God's Heavenly lights
I see your face shining bright.

Mother dear, I miss you so—
My heart aches even tho
I sense your every presence here with me,
Ever so close to touch and see.

Come here, come here and take my pen—
Use my hand to express yourself
And live through me again,
For you shall always live on through poetry and song—
For you were so romantic and young at heart—
I'll never be alone. . .

God came to take you as you slept
Here in my bedroom,
Where I wept, for I knew
I would never see you again, physically,
But you'll always be in my heart spiritually.

Tell Dad I love him and miss him, too;
I long for the day I'll be there with you,
There beyond the Evening Star
Guiding us here from afar,
Blessing each and every one—
Here a daughter—there a son.

Yes, you're there with the angels in Heaven,
Yet here on Earth amongst us seven,
for you bore three before me and three after:
Two boys, four girls, brought you pain and laughter.
One was stillborn;
She's there with you;
I, your daughter, broke your hearts,
But loved you true.

Oh, How I remember our roaming through the meadows
Early in the morn,
Hand in hand,
Picking daisies till we were weary and worn.
Then we'd set under the old weeping willow tree,
Where you'd cuddle me close and sing to me.

And I know you'll always be with me
For I see you there—
There amidst the daffodils
As I sit by the brook at the
Foot of the hills.

As I stroll through the wood beneath the fall pine tree,
I hear your voice, (Your singing)
And you whisper softly to me—
"Don't cry, don't cry, my dear,
For I'll always be with you—
Right here, right here in your heart."

THE SONG OF THE BIRD

Beautiful, marvelous creature divine,
How I adore your music sublime. . .
Whence thou cometh or whither thou goeth
Your shrill notes thrill me from highest to lowest!
Those sweet liquid tunes seem to lift up my soul
To lofty heights that we cannot control;
Your song is a melody from above;
It fills me with goodness, gladness, and love.
Sing out, oh thou bird, I never get weary
Of hearing your songs; they make me feel cheery!
I never feel melancholy or blue
Because I'm continually listening to you.

WEAR A SMILE

A smile is as essential as our everyday attire;
It's truly providential if one you can inspire.
Awaken in the morning with a smile upon your face
You'll soon find it adorning someone's countenance with grace.
True mirth is as contagious as a drowsy, sleepy yawn;
It's really advantageous; start smiling with the dawn.
A laugh is like a tonic to a weary, sickly soul;
Try to be harmonic, let laughter be your goal!

* * *

KIND WORDS, KIND THOUGHTS

Riches, gold, and luxuries are nice,
Although they are associates of vice.
All aren't happy possessing these things;
Kind words, kind thoughts, true happiness brings.
Kind words each day and a big hearty smile
Put joy in one's heart; makes life worthwhile.
Breathe prayers and sing as oft as ye will;
Contentment will be the reward and thrill!

THE GARDEN

You have knelt here where your altars are invalid,
among the lilacs and the fences and the sheep;
with your head upon your palms
you wait on benches—
pray for respite while the silence bids you sleep.

There were dreams left on the benches in this garden,
by the yew trees, near the hedgerow, in your time—
dreams that ride the rain with sea gulls
in the autumn,
and elude you in the ruins of your rhyme.

Between the questions and the answers there were moments
far removed from all the distances of time;
but the moments were but moments
which grew vaguer,
while you sipped off all the vinegar from the wine.

You're a watcher, an observer; you fit nowhere
in the garden or in April's gentle scheme;
you're a cross between the sunshine
and the raindrops—
in your hand a withered violet and your dream.

So you sit there saying nothing, simply sitting;
laughing children in the distance pay no heed
to you returning to your garden
long remembered,
cursing neither sunshine nor the rain.

SUMMER STORM

The gale wind hath blown for three hours now,
Swirling the gray mist o'er the bare-swept plain.
The sky was turbulent with ominous storm clouds;
The wind lifted leaves, long dead, from their graves.

Willows danced to the gale; their wailing I heard,
So silently I listened and waited for rain.
And said was brought forth by a lone night bird;
Plummeting the mountains, the valleys and plains.

I glanced to the mountain peaks, hidden by cloud,
Long-scorched by the merciless sun,
Now drenched by the rain, beneath their black shroud,
Which they could not shun.

The turbulent stream its froth did spew
Upon each sodden bank.
The forceful wind each wave pursued
Through dismal night so dank.

As I turned to part the rain did still,
So poised to wait, and heard
A sound, yet sweet, did send a chill:
The cry of a lone night bird.

DOUGHBOY

Once a single thought begins to form
on mind of loneliness confined. . .
rows of sorrows stand in line,
marching reason out of time.

Taught to leave the thinking
to the leader. . .never blinking;
hope retards. . .begins its sinking—
raw resentments slowly storm.

Within a newness needs to form—
a singleness of thought to come alive!
Making hope and faith to strive
at killing hate. .turning love to be the drive!

All around need repeats!
Others duplicate the soul's retreat!
Sound the warning of defeat!. . .
Trust in God!. . .for victory born!

* * *

PROGRESS

Mow a path across the horizon. . .
Seek to cut a swath so smooth
that when others seek to follow you
they'll find you've cut their work in two.

245

THE GAMBLER AND THE PAIR OF DICE

D-Day
> I can't believe you'd wait in line
> To shake the dotted two!
> I fear you'll win
> The spotted cloak—
> The over-bloodied spue!
>
> Will you be wise to take this thing
> If luck to you bestows?
> The martyr's wrap
> You've won before—
> And felt its troubled woes.
>
> The dice turn dark upon this throw;
> The night descends upon the day.
> An omen of disgrace I feel
> To gamble for this robe—
> Resist, my friend, I pray!
>
> You've set your heart upon this goal
> To wear the fellow's clothes.
> Are you aware of this man's cause—
> Of what he leaves behind?
> Remember what he chose!
>
> You banter of the self-same talk,
> These around you boast;
> Yet in the speech of this one man,
> Of God
> He speaks the most!

I've not a mite of want to be involved
In this, your gambling vice,
To own his ware
To even share
The throwing of these dice!

A.D.-Day
Another pair of dice are thrown today
As men go passing by.
They've tried to win
A whited robe
That caused a man to die!

The dotted pair of well-worn sides
Bespeaks of little gain.
What gamble is there left to try
To rob the King of Kings?

I'll be involved, but gamble not!
Receive His sacrifice!
A robe like his
He's shared with me
To wear in Paradise!

"BUT. . .HOW DO YOU KNOW?"

How do I know, dear heart,
    if there is a God?
I know when I filter my fingers
    through the sod,
then reach a hand upon
    the grass I trod.
I know. . .I know. . .
    there is a God.

How do I know, dear heart,
    there is a God?
Within me beats a pulse. . .
    an inner live facade,
where a Father meets me gently
    with staff and rod,
There I know. . .I know. . .
    there is a living God.

Will you know him too, dear heart?
    Is it your wish to know?
Look around you and you will see. . .
    his mammoth, majestic show!
Could all this be happenstance. . .
    this, by nobody to us bestow?
Consider. . .consider. . .
    Would you know?

Will you know him, too, deart heart?
    Is it your wish to know?
You have but to ask the wind
    of his Spirit to blow. . .
To come by, and let you feel
    his Presence glow. . .
To consider. . .to consider. . .
    there is a God—to know.

SORROWS OF THE NIGHT

There are those who lie restless,
tossing, fretting. . .blaming others
for their troubled sleep.
Wherefore does it follow
for us to know. . . God's intent?

There are those who succor defeat,
relentlessly tying knots on errors,
so folks can't go beyond
the place they claim is theirs. . .not God's.

So, feeding on oblique abstinence,
failure succeeds. . .solidifies—
racing forward and upward,
futilely—
bracing shamefully. . .against God.

God, teach them the art of loving. . .
Unwind the tangled scenes. . .
the road to faith. . .show them the map.
Melt away the hardening darkness
toward you. . .and us.

* * *

TRANSITION

Soft shades of night—
douse the vivid. . .
restrain the livid. . .
Igniting the moon for light.

GOD PROVIDES HIS COVERINGS

CELESTIAL: Clouds over warm earth
Darkness over weary sleepers
CREATION: Grass on summer soils
Snow on bare cold ground
BODY BEAUTY: Hair to frame our face reflection
Clothes to grace our outer view
PEOPLED-PEACE: Government for group guidelines
Management for merriment and milestones
INNER INVESTMENT: The garment of God
Faith, hope, love and truth.
SPIRITUAL SPACE: Salvation. . .Jesus
His Holy Presence. . .Prayer

* * *

FULL-FILLED

Men drove God out
they thought;
but God noted their emptiness
and graciously returned,
and brought
His LOVE.

POOR LEOPARD

Poor leopard,
With your sad green eyes—
Pacing the solitary confines
Of your cage,
So full of sorrow,
So full of mournful reproach
For those who made you captive.
You, of the wild spirit,
The restless heart,
You were meant
To stalk through jungles;

I feel the deep hurt
Within your cold green eyes,
I know your eager longing,
Your deep urge to be free;
For I, too, am a free spirit
That brooks no captivity,
No bonds—

We are kindred,
You and I,
We have but one wish:
To break the bonds that bind us,
You, to roam again
Your wild, wild kingdom,
And I to break
The cage men call the world,
And know INFINITY!

SKY PAINTING

"You will paint the sky today,"
The heavenly command was given
To the youngest angels,
The two-year, three-year,
Four-year and five-year-olds.

"What colors may we have?"
Asked the little angels,
"Why, all the colors you wish!
Help yourselves
To the heavenly paints!"

So into rose and blue,
And gold and green,
And royal purple,
The youngest angels
Dipped their brushes.

They raced across the sky,
Brushing the beautiful colors
In broad strokes, swirls,
While all the colors flowed together
In breathless beauty!

And that evening
People everywhere
Looked up at the sky and said,
"What a glorious sunset!"
But they never knew
That the cherub angels had painted it!

SUMMER IS LOVE

The songs of summer come to an end
As the leaves of autumn begin to descend;
And the warmth and love that I once remember
like the setting sun that gleams in September
Fills my heart with strife and grief
As the summer dies with every falling leaf;
Strife and grief on the fringe of pain
like the morning dew is to the evening rain.
For now winter makes its forbidden call
And the colorless trees say goodbye to fall;
My lingering soul with hope grows limber
As a noontime snow sprinkles late December
And the sky stays so gray, blurry, and chilled
As my dying hopes struggle to live.
But suddenly the snow begins to melt away
And the songs of birds announce the coming day.
In the clear blue sky there is a sign of love
As a brisk spring shower falls from above,
with the peace and happiness it brings to mind
I know that summer can't be far behind.

* * *

THE ULTIMATE JOURNEY

I tossed a pebble off the eroding
bank
And watched as it skipped congruously
across the still water,
Only to sink into an undercurrent
of eternity. . .

253

A SIGN OF JOY

So peaceful is the meadow
With it's fluorescent smell of spring—
So happy is the morning
As a chorus of birdies sing—
And a noontime rain
Which comes trinkling from above
Seems to touch my shrilling lips
And quench my thirsty soul with love. . .

* * *

DON'T PASS IT ON

Say, Brother! Don't pass it on!!
Don't pass on your sleepless nights,
Your endless journey filled with agony
and haunting nightmares. . .
Don't pass on your useless mind, murderous
escapades, and your bleeding eyes;
Don't pass on your heartbreak, your sorrow and your
Nodding head;
Keep your addicting needle, vein-busting syringe
And your self-inflicted genocide,
Losing scope on reality; losing scope on life,
For you're a volunteer slave, cowering before the
plague of the white death,
Falling into a bottomless pit somewhere between
time and space,
Chasing a fleeting star: A star that descends beyond
the metaphysical world—
So keep your chains and shackles—for liberation is
our bag now. . .

SUMMER IN THE CITY

As I greet another summer in the city,
The things I see bring tears of pity:
Children playing barefooted in the street,
Roaming around with nothing to eat;
Winos bumming for just one more,
Inflation, recession are both in store.
Mothers up to their necks in debt,
Praying for the man with the welfare check.
And the air ain't fit for a baby to breathe;
The rats don't know how to take a reprieve.
Politicians are saying everything is all right
It's just that the budget is a little too tight.
Still junkies O.D. in abandoned lots,
And people ain't friendly 'cause it's so
damn hot.

* * *

THE RIVER

. . . . .Throbbing and bobbing
On its pre-charted course;
. . . . .Gushing and flowing
Through a sequence of glittering blueness;
. . . . .Moving and grooving
To the sounds of time. . .
For there is perseverance in the river.
So much beauty there
. . . . .Enchanting and elegant,
Bringing in the serene air from
Yesteryear's dream. . .

255

EQUALITY

The Negro, Indian, and Jew
Are human beings through and through,
As even I and you and you,
They do not—should not—
Ask for more or less
Then life can give—
Yes, to live good lives as worthwhile citizens,
And also give with pride as men who strive
For equality of self, and life and limb.
God made all men as brothers;
No one human being better then another.

* * *

MY PEN, MY SWORD

It is said that the pen is mightier than the sword.
If this is so I do not know;
Sometimes my pen is feather-light
And my words sound gay and bright;
There are other times I feel
That this life is not for real;
Nor is it all sweet comedy.
I feel it is a drama, eloquently deep and grand,

And so many things seem preordained,
As the lines engraved upon the hand.
If I use my pen as if a sword,
To pursue those ever-present beastly forces,

I pray, my Lord, guide this pen-word sword
As lightning striking motion,
For thunder not alone begot;
With rumbling grumbling notions
Its brilliants feared and shared,
From combustion to conclusion.

BELOVED

Beloved, it was your cheerful smile
    that delighted me when I was sad;
It was your tender, loving kiss that
    sparked a light in my wounded heart;
All my fears and sorrows vanished with
    one touch of your hand;
It was your deep love that gave me
    hope when I was in the dark.
Though oftentimes we can't have the
    things we want most,
Or enjoy life's very best without a
    single cost,
Yet none could be more beautiful than
    a love so true;
Your love, my dearest, is the best gift,
    I want most from you.
For you are the sunshine and water that
    nourished my dying love,
The rainbow that appeared after a storm
    in the sky above,
A tree, forever firm, but standing resilient
    amidst worries and strifes;
Beloved, you are the long-lost paradise
    I've searched for—all my life.

LET ME THINK OF THEE

Let me think of thee each day of the year,
    Let me think of thee as I say my
        daily prayer.
Let me think of thee when no one else would do,
    Let me think of thee after a day's hard
        labor is through.
Let me think of thee when the moon is new,
    Let me think of thee though the orange
        blossoms are few—
Let me think of thee when night meets day,
    Let me think of thee when your hair
        turns gray.
Let me think of thee in the change of seasons,
    Let me think of thee for a lot of reasons.
Let me think of thee when you doubt my love,
    Let me think of thee as dark clouds hover in
        the skies above.
Let me think of thee should the world ever
        forget you—
    Let me think of thee, beloved, my whole
        life through.

THE OTHER MAN

It's not how many handsprings we may turn from day to day,
But the smile we give a fellow that counts, along our way.
It isn't worthy to be famous if all we do or care for is
        ourselves;
We must remember first that the other fellow's there.
So share your courage and convictions with him,
Make room for his expression to be free,
For he's as great a fellow in the sight of God as even
        you and me.

* * *

A MOTHER'S RESPONSE

My darling, you're the little one your parents waited for,
Sent to us alone from Heaven with all God's love,
For us to guide and cherish our lives through forevermore.
There's nothing more worthy or more purely fair
Than the time-written memories that you planted there.
You captured our hearts, dear, that beat just for thee
A blessing from God to your daddy and me.
I'll now search the Scriptures until I discover
God's will, for me to be worthy to be called
        "Your dear Mother."

VANNELLI FAMILY TREE

I don't know how the family tree came about,
Except perhaps from a French tribe of that name in
Normandy;
In 1783, one of my ancestors, Leonardo, no doubt,
Honored the Italian branch with Lodavico, Michele and
Giovanni.

From these forebears came Great-Grandfather
Cresenzia;
Tall and blue-eyed, he came to America from Abouzzi.
He had a wife, short and dark, called Angelina;
Five feet one, she lived till eighty.

My grandpa and grandma were young, in Minnesota,
When they settled in St. Paul in the nineteenth century,
Coming here by way of Quebec, Canada—
A proud hardy stock from sunny Italy.

Strangers—they met and married here,
Among the first to live in a non-Italian neighborhood,
Pioneers in sending their children to school there,
In search of freedom and a livelihood.

My father, a native of the land of the free,
My mother, a Wojtkiewicz, a Polish beauty from
Wisconsin.
With my brothers enriching new blood into the family tree;
Now I must add the names of my little Tommy and Kristin.

INDEPENDENCE

The trend today is to be independent,
Different, self-dependent.
I stand on the street corner
Observing the people.

The sun shines brightly over the hilltop.
Its beams glisten off the sides
Of white houses.

The streets are filled with cars
And people hurriedly going on their way.
The weather is warm and pleasant;
The people are warm and pleasant.

Suddenly the brightness of the sun
Is covered by dark, unyielding clouds;
The rain falls, the wind blows.
The streets are filled with cars
And people hurriedly going on their way.
The weather is dull and irritable;
The people are dull and irritable.

As suddenly as it began, the rain stops;
The wind is no more.
The people are warm and pleasant once again.

The trend today is to be independent.
True independence comes only
When we can overcome
The rain, the wind, and the clouds.

THE VISION

The soft winds splashed
quietly upon my face,
  Standing alone without a
  trace of humanity;

  and a vision spoke to me.

  Soft was her voice
  as the gentle rains,

  Kind was the touch
  that relieved my pain,

  Gentle were her movements
  as a star-spangled space.

My vision glided upward,
Through the trees
  and back again.

Extending over watery shadows
    and back again,
    my vision smiled at me.

    Her eyes were painted
    with a thousand smiles,

    Her hand combed my hair
    like the wind,

    Her voice was a natural symphony.

We rode the wind happily together
searching out all eternity;
    for you see
        my love was my vision,
        The white-winged dove
        and me.

Thom Lutz

LOVE: OUR ONLY SAVIOR

Through our greed we
become blinded,
> And through our blindness
> become wicked.

Through our wickedness we
become mournful,
> and through our tears
> become selfish.

Through our gains we
become selfishly sad,
> and through our sadness
> become happy once again.

Through the eyes and ears,
and the sights of sound we
> travel through the colourful
> array of mixed emotion.

Through time we
become burdened,
> and through our burdens
> become timeless.

Through our hate we
become spiteful,
> and through our spite
> return to the robes of
> love once more.

So it is that
> Love
> > is our only Savior.

THE VISION

Within the vision
Is the smile,
Enchanting
lips spreading synthetic sensuality
Beyond the wallowing reality
Of cooperation.
Adding stature to style,
Inciting nervy suppositions,
Dressing the mind with naked pleasures while
Wearing wanton masks.

　　　　The vision
Held close to the bosom, like a dying child,
Cannot be realized.
It withers in the drought of dispassionate
Ghetto streets. Its petals fall
On reservations and on the crushed
Cockroached plaster of dirty Chicano walls.

The vision stalls the visitor:
Nihilimus.
But the dead still crawl
And the living ache,
And those who have, have;
And those who have not
Hate impatiently.
They bear the self-effacing weight
And wait
To burn the dead and withered
Vision and dust it from
Their memory,
And fling it on the wind.

TEAR

Yes, it hurts,
Being black,
But you must remember that
there is a peculiarity about the mind:
it forgets the ache of pain.
Memories linger and fade and
pain, like rain,
condensates and evaporates—
is felt, and if forgotten,
is the fate of snow in springtime.
So you get up every morning, anyway,
And you persevere.
It is a cumbersome task:
Getting up; being black;
Smiling and being smiled at
while shit is smeared
in your face.
Hating and all the time feeling
God-damned.

Yes, it hurts.
Being black
is like not being white,
if you can imagine that.
It's like being colored
by stereotype and redundant myths;
Like being based
with hot tar and feathered with ridicule.
Tar-baby; bossed, bastardized, and debased by Tarzan
Obsessions of white superiority.
Being black is being bound
to be an American
when everyone else is
free to *be*.
Being black
is being made, molded, manufactured, and motherfucked.
Yes, it hurts. . .

GENESIS

Silhouetted against a golden moon
She stood
Alone,
Watching the ship sail ahead of the breeze.
She fell to her knees,
Simultaneously pounding
And clutching her pregnant mound,
Crying
Because she could not go;
Crying because she could not sail
Inside the beautiful ship
Upon the sea,
with the white-faced man who
Had fascinated her
And her family
With bright red laced velvet scarves
And pearls and gold
And incense.
Her tears streamed down
Her ebony face, streamed
As the Congo
Through the darkness of her homeland.
And she kneeled
Alone,
With her dark arms now outspread to merge
With the sky,
One hand clenched into a fist,
One hand clenching a knife—
A bloody knife—
Bleeding the blood of
Her belly.

H. S. McFarland

HOPE

Encrouched, the danger of philosophies
Conflicting, fill the air with messages.
May I not silently sit this one out
Lamenting, talking to my Ego, gout?

What now affords me license to dispense
A near-forgotten hope of pure nonsense,
A hope that yet one day this Earth shall be
A unity of bright eternity?

Ah, ranging on the spectrum of the light,
May I in flattery clothe my slim delight
That there I see a flicker dying quite
Of malnutrition in the late, late night?

Hope *does* remain within the human breast
Till all the lights have thus been put to rest.

THIS, TOO, SHALL PASS!

When theory conficts with practice prone
The method of arranger should be known,
But each time principle is press'd, alas!
Arranger would declaim: "This, too, shall pass!"

And when, obviously, a fad draws near
The pressure of community affair
Calls forth the faddist who, a pretty lass—
The lass explains: "This, too, shall pass!"

Arrived the day some ragged rowdies came
With sticks, with stones, with bombings and with flame—
To give account, from citadel of grass,
Rowdies replied en masse: "This, too, shall pass!"

This, too, shall pass! our pillaged, burnt-out towns,
Rebuilt some day—for now, they are in ruins!

H. S. McFarland

MOOD

As borne on the breakers lilies of white,
   Geese in their ermine o'ershadow the sight,
   Gulls up above and doves soaring high,
   Tinge the horizon and mottle the sky.

As stars on thought's fringes play on the mind,
   Images merging as tassels unwind,
   Circles endeavor to fit into squares,
   Such is the flair that banishes cares.

As fancy, the abstract leader supreme,
   Lord of the lantern eternally keen,
   Buoys the spirit thru storms and great strife,
   So aid follows flight to infinite scene.

This is a mood of personal choice,
Lighting, highlighting its motto: Rejoice!

COMPANION

'Twas only but a morning walk he took,
Nothing irregular, but then he shook
As tho someone had placed restraining hand,
Gently designed to have him understand.

The opposite effect came nigh in force
As he in circles saw no one, of course,
Fostered by fright, he took to flight, recoil'd—
Composed, sketchy imagination foil'd.

But 'twas not as he deemed it would have been—
A sprig experience in a spur of thought;
The afternoon's performance repeat spots
The vivid packet morning's stroll had bought:

"To him who stops to read," the poster said,
"Thou art not alone—companion overhead!"

CHEERFULNESS

Pleasantry indulged in now and then
Is a splendid tonic for women and men.

Unless we indulge in a little *mirth,*
What can life be really worth?

Your *countenance* is always on display
So endeavor to make it bright and gay.

A spirit of *animation* is fine,
And those who possess it with radiance shine.

When with enthusiasm you *greet* a friend,
A gracious compliment to him you extend.

On Father's Day make him *glad.*
After all he is your Dad.

She bubbles over with vigor and glee.
Her *ebullient* nature is something to see.

With *amiable* associates we feel at ease,
Because they are friendly and aim to please.

With horns, and bells, and *hilarious* cheer,
The crowd in Times Square salutes the New Year.

Her gracious personality charms
As she *welcomes* her guests with open arms.

THE STORMY NIGHT

Yellow points,
lit cottage and farm;
pinprick blotted fields
    on audible pall
of mild September black
heaving on gale.

Some in view, fixed. One
through seethed woods
flickers, shuts, glows on, looks
caught up in the sounding
unseen drama, spearclash of trees'
embattled torment.
    Wink and beckon enthreshed,
on set gleam's real,
    flare
a wildfire sense of moment.

Mind may finger fancies
on these lights, purpose
in houses, and one knows illusion.
Knots it, too,
of the whole thing-in-itself light
feigning to meet
for a glance, an evening, lean
to presence, steady
outside self.

But one cries a reach beyond
happening, people even,
and may joy at the power
of a stormy night to conjure
darkened being groping out,
and seeming something
    answering.

Scruncheons (Canada), Vol. 1, No. 2.

* * *

BYPASS

A last bulldozer, clawing, snarled its bites
of soil down slopes; blue-reeking tarmac
was hot-ironed on; the new straightened road
ramped up from the bent bridge in the valley
was finished in April.

Crude in the spring landscape,
inverted nail-paring of earth raw-red,
skid for cars going this way and that way;
Later they sowed the sides with grass seed.

And in September, astonishing, there
in tired fields, leaves rattling toward fall,
the grass grew as spring, emerald-vivid
and shining as grasses in April,

smelling of April, in autumn already
far distant, of startings and freshness
at time of check and suspension and ache
for the spring, aging, as I walked
in that strange coexistence.

United Kingdom (England), Vol. XX, No. 107.

CAUSE OF THUNDER

In tight neat hush of hotel lounge,
in smart university town,
the buttoned conversations sibilate
and drop phrases overhearable:
correctly tone important social stance
or acceptable sense.

"What d'ya learn in colleges—
religion, truth, philosophy?"
Too-loud burst from a man at the bar:
stiff-swaying, unstoppable, mariner eyes
in glittering swing for prey:
wild, shabby, mad or bum-drunk,
craving talk.

"Are you philosophers?"
People drink up faster,
look at watches, rise and leave.
"You go. You have the answers.
I must speak with you.
Can't you say anything?"
Singled out, I too, polite,
make my excuse,
feeling, like them, my right
to private pass with truth.

And after
in the street,
            knew I was less than king.

Canadian Author and Bookman, Vol. 47, No. 3.

EMBROIDERY OF VERACITY

Embroidered in my soul may there ever be the acceptance of
        your will,
that should the winds grow, there'd be in my heart a still
Of Trust,
That your Love's generosity may never be taken unseen.

* * *

I SET MY LOVE FREE
UNKNOWINGLY

So busy in the coil of things that can be,
stands the remnant of a captivated fragmented dream,
Was it me?
I set my love free in unrecorded time; the calendar bore
no date.
The mere weight of fate dwindles upon the spindle,
a basis of bias silence,
as the myriad affluence suspends amidst a happiness jubilee,
and unknowingly waits upon nights lingering *sine die,*
I cannot help but feel as a magent of vacuum,
amidst the hum of past madrigals,
kneeling in past suns.

I set my love free—unknowingly—
as one can lose a token;
marked words spoken and spent,
to bear the mark of their significance,
always with the countenance of gentle innocence.

Farewell, my requisite love,
as the silent still of the suspended rain
muffles the reciting of your name
to the reducing sound
of
a
breath.

CHURCH SICKNESS

Old Sister Menefee got "church sickness";
She say God is her medicine. . .
seems like she should have had an overdose by now.

Just as if a doctor had prescribed it, she's in there,
down there, around there, prayin', prayin', prayin',
Mornin' doses, afternoon and evening doses. . .
Seems like Sister Menefee get sick a-prayin' so much.
Well, that's what I call it—"church sickness."

Old Sister Menefee just eats religion, sleeps religion,
talks religion, feels religion,
And if you ask her, "Sister Menefee, what does Orthodoxy
mean?"
she couldn't tell you—
All that religion and can't spell *"theeology."*

What you think about someone knowin' the gospel, and
can't spell a simple word like "truth";
Sayin' she Saves, but don't know what "sanctimonious" means.

I saw Old Sister Menefee—Friday, I believe it was. . .
We was talkin' and she come tellin' me she ain't never
heard tell of the Thirty-nine Articles, The Confessions
of Augsberg, or The Tridentines Decrees. . .
Po' Old Sister Menefee. . .

i won't call him abominable said James Baldwin
because he is a long way from being a snowman

that little loathsome child,
looking nasty and very vile,
such a disgusting little brat—
nose running, face black.

* * *

A NOT SELF-SINNERED CHILD

God never screwed my mama
and i ain't none of God's chillin'.
i am the sun of the devil
and my daddy's one helluva man. . .

* * *

THE PREACHER AND THE SINNER IN CHURCH

talking rapidly and indistinctively,
unintelligible chatter of total destruction. . .

hearing indirectly, listening eagerly,
anxiously waiting for the end. . .

*the big, bad, blazing sun looking down on it all—a single
and separated entity.

NEGROES AND WOMEN BECOME CITIZENS

Our social culture moves along slow,
But if given enough time it may make a go.
It is making full-fledged citizens of Negroes and women.

I must confess that of some things the men have made a mess.
Pollution, wars, and waste
Should be changed with great haste.

The rule of a matriarchy may have to return—
Then wouldn't the men's faces burn?
We may have to return to a matriarchate
To become culturally efficient before it is too late.

* * *

JEALOUS CRITICS

Pay no attention to jealous, deprecating
Critics who are trying to change your view.
By the process of comparison they don't measure up to you.
View your own behavior objectively;
Be sure that you are right.
Caustic, jealous remarks are weapons with which they fight.
Their jealous, caustic remarks will eventually boomerang;
They will become the victims of their own harangue.
Just give them enough rope and themselves they will hang.

DESERT INDIAN LOVE SONG

Stars of night, pale moonlight.
Desert space hides your face.
Warm winds blow sands like snow,
You will know I love you so!

My love flies through the skies;
Spirit voice, lover's choice
Speaks to me: "Love, like sea,
Deep and wide, strong like tide,
I am by your side."

Stars of night, pale moonlight,
Desert space hides your face.
Soft winds blow clouds like snow,
You will know I loved you so!
I—westward, westward—go.

* * *

A DAFFODIL

A yellow daffodil blooms upon my window sill,
Spreading its golden glow afar,
Catching a light from the Christmas Star.

* * *

FUNERAL FLOWERS

Damp and dewy funeral flowers
          Weep upon thy grave.
Soon they will fade and die,
Oh, beloved, as will I—
          My heart, upon thy grave.

281

THE ENDLESS SEA OF TOMORROWS

Do you remember all the golden aeons of your yesterdays?
The romantic past of your carbon atoms and chemical mixtures
Coupling to forge the present you? You do not? Strange. You
Were *somewhere.* "Nothing comes from nothing," Mr. Socrates said.
Your father and mother did not conceive you. They were the crude
Instruments that brought you into the world. You did not create
Yourself; if you had you would remember it: a man values
his toys.
You were plucked from the pregnant air, but you had a beginning.
If you don't remember your beginning, your yesterdays, it seems
Strange to believe you will remember today, when you embark on
That endless sea of tomorrows that borders upon Mirror Worlds
Unbounded by Space and Time. Had you thought of that? No?
Then I fear you are one of St. John's "doubly dead," for thought
is the highest form of action, and action is the highest form of life.
Action and Change are the only realities. The grave will not honor or reward
You. "There is no other world," Emerson said. "Here or nowhere is
The whole fact." Christ said, "The Kingdom of Heaven is on earth."

If this be true, does it not follow that earth is where God is
Being built? That we mortals are the Immortal's work
battalion?
You agree? Then why does Man make his earth, his heaven, a
blood-stained
Slaughterhouse where he kills for fun and sport? Is it because
he
Is cursed with a death wish and is determined to exterminate
his species?
Or is it because of the childish notion that man hates his
Father and
Wants to kill God? If so, man is deluding himself—not the
Almighty.
God was here first. He will survive, whether Man chooses to
do so or not.

BENEATH HAWAII'S SKIES

People walk in awe of
Bright skies with shaded blues,
Marshmallow clustered clouds,
Sunshine, instant rain,
Happening all at once. . .

Races from all walks of life
Live in harmony, we born of the soil
Alive with memories of times we watched the
Art of fishing from the sea,
Picking seaweed from the rocks,
Waves splashing kisses on our cheeks,
Sun play hide and seek with clouds
While rain drops in between. . .

Day to day doors opened wide. . .
Once, while in natural state,
Papas, Mamas, friends were one.
Work seemed more like play
In the shadows of the past;
New and frightened world came fast.
Pulling strength we knew not how to use
Till we reached back to hold Jewels of our past;

Know truth inherited with fact.

They taught appreciation of all things,
Like dew appearing crystals on the lawn,
Undivided invisible ring of love;
Mostly how to live as one
Beneath Hawaii's skies

?

What can I do? When I cannot do?
Should I stop? Destroy? Die?
Be born again? Could I?

IDEA

Sometimes you can build up,
Sometimes you have to destroy
To become free,
To begin again.

Sorry, all you have done is gone;
You must start anew.

Perhaps, begin with a point,
Maybe a line
Or a color,
Only a touch.
Should we try?
Or not?
Or is it better to let the idea
Remain an idea,
An idea without materialization?

THE SEA

The sea, the waves; stormy, wild;
Inescapably over the land;
Blue, green; white foam over the black rocks;
Actions, wild, strong; the waves, the sea.

CONCERN FOR MAN—SILENTLY VANISHING

A new life—a new son;
The sun shines bright
Man with his knowledge
Offering—giving a helping hand
All feeling the song—clear—
Like a bird as the day begins,
All basking in the sweet aroma
Like a flowering bud.
A new son—a new mother—
With breath rolling smoothly
Like the ripples of clear water—filled with assurance.
Man's knowledge—man's helping hand—within reach. . .
Willing to guide him—protect him. . .
The clouds carry months to years—
Eighteen—a new man.
Suddenly, alone, reaching out,
A mother weeps.
Man's helping hand beyond reach,
Man and his knowledge have rolled with the clouds
Man's concern—silently vanishing—
They fade away—disappear—
Too distant to hear—to see. . .
The sun shines dim;
Less birds to sing;
Flowers weep—their buds are few;
Drowning waters cry—no room to breathe;
Heard only are the sounds of war,
Calling out to a once new son,
Now a new man. . .
Eighteen—Alone. . .

IN DUE TIME, YOU TOO

I woke up one morning and climbed a tree.
"Get down, you foolish child, or you won't live to see three,"
My mother said to me.
Money tucked in my pocket, and off to the store,
Laughing and skipping, skipping and laughing,
"Come join me, friends, and candy we'll buy."
We ate and we skipped, we ate and we laughed,
"Oh, you foolish child, no milk, no bread, candy instead.
        Thank goodness I have one of you and not three,"
My mother said to me.
Dressed in blue, my hair in a bow,
Prom night had come, I was ready to go.
Fell down a stair, lost my shoe,
Tripped my date and broke his foot.
"You foolish child, how will you make it to twenty-three?"
My mother said to me.
I woke up one morning, I was thirty-three;
It wasn't the birds, or the crickets that called to me,
I looked out the window and what did I see?
My three sons, all climbing a tree
"Oh my goodness, what ever happened to me?"
A mother of three, I said to me.

TO HOLD GOD'S HAND

There is a cozy look within the room
As my window frames the fury of a storm;
Trees are twisting, agonized by the wind
As it opens its mouth and blows fiercely again.

I hear the birds as they huddle together,
Their singing seems changed to a call;
They sound frightened, without a place to go—
Feathers fly at the gust of a blow. . .

Now the daylight dims, tho it's early morn;
Dark clouds are churning in the sky,
Petals of flowers shatter to the ground,
Lightning flashes, heavy rains come down.

The echo of my footsteps grows louder,
My heart pounds as I pace the floor;
Thoughts turn to the helplessness of man—
Prayerfully, I reach to hold God's hand.

* * *

LOVE

As my emotions rise to crest
A suckling babe is at my breast,
What truer love could I find
Than flesh of flesh, a part of mine.

LORD TOMORINO

"Aye my lad, thou but to grow; fortunes will be thine, I know."
Repeated words of long ago, spoken by my Lord Tomorino.
"Be sure as day is light and comes each dawn for those with sight—
Thou will attain thy birthright," so spoke my Lord Tomorino.
"Behold the day! thine cup refill with wisdom, truth, and wariness.
Be wise in all thou say and hear;
Be wise in where thou go; thou go with fear.
Be wary, if thou come and go and in the light perceive
A thing; thine eyes deceive. Behold! Beware! thy friends and foe.
Beware lest when thou speak, the truth be twisted or will reek
When returned, and thou seek a friend, but find a foe—
Beware, my son, when day is done—beware of dragons in the dark
Lest while thou sleep these serpents creep,
When with the dawn, thy life be gone;
When friends come to see a friend, find naught but a memory.
Behold! when thou thy fortune seek; when thou see one that thou buy three
And in return, sell one for three—Be honest as honor can be.
Beware while thou do look around, lest things trodden on the ground
Be rarer than gold found, in purse or treasury.
Be wise! Beware! Behold!
Be wise, do not abide—but come a time to seek a mate— choose wisely,
Not left to fate. . .In time, thou will find
Loving memory will bind. Behold! Beware! Be wise!
Be wise and likewise be—as they would—that thou treat he;
Be not a foe but be a friend; be not a follower, but set the trend;

Be generous, loyal, and kind—and thou will have peace of
mind;
Remember well for all time, thee—that men but mortals be."
So shall it be and so it will eternally.
Like mortal men—a mortal he—walked unafraid.
And in the Fall, when brown leaves fall, beseeched by all
to stay away
That fatal day—he dared to ride.
Seems but today—my Lord rode hence
His only weapon for defense, his personality.
As they neared, his entourage, cheered by the crowd,
My Lord did recompense, in voice loudly intoned—
"Remember thee—remember well—if there but a little be,
If thou get some, it would be more than before.
The little plus this little some be better than none;
If thou add more to some, richer than before thou be;
Take some; share with one poorer than thee,
Both enriched will be.
For selfishness breeds jealousy and hate—and hate endures.
With but one mouth thou can't eat more;
With but two hands thou can't hold more;
With but one life thou need no more than he,
And men despair with lost dreams of spring.
Does not the robin's song joyful tidings bring
To each and every living thing?
So I beg today, for thee to pray that fortune's winds prevail,
Fulfill the hopes and dreams of men that they may live
without fear."
With this—betrayed—my Lord Tomorino was slayed—
Prolonged silence did ensue
And through the crowd, and through my head,
The thought, the dread—
Lord Tomorino is dead.
As with the turning of the tide a traitor, with a friend,
will ride
And ride that day he did. This traitorous rogue, up to
the end,

Had been a friend to my Lord. His only sin to atone
Was aspiration to the throne—whereat sat my Lord.
(Even today, it grieves the cord—to speak of him, whom
I adored.)
No silver tongue, no mighty sword can withhold the hands
of time;
Or stay the tolling of the bell, when time has passed.
But once outcast, a rogue rescinds his love; forgets time
and fear;
Learns to hate, and casts his fate with winds that blow,
Scattering near and far evil thoughts and evil ways;
Allies himself with one who slays.
So amid that crowd an ally hid, with gun in hand,
Deranged with greed and hate (his soul in hell will rot)
He can't think straight, except to do as he is bid;
To raise his hand and shoot my Lord.
At the ringing of the shot—we could but stand awed,
amazed,
And gaze with mouths agape, while he made his escape.
When sands of time no hope renew, and lovers bemoan their
doom
Too late, we learn that irony of fate can choose
Who will win and who will lose.
But why must good die young, and evil decay as age?
Relentless time, what is thy rate or gauge?
The solemn days went swiftly by; long since death did
discharge his loan,
The trumpet's blast—his coming home.
Where whirlwinds blow there he will lie, forevermore he'll
be nearby
Where swallows nest he'll come to rest at evening tide;
Where waters flow, at sunset glow, you've but to look within
my heart,
Where'er I go—forevermore, will be my father,
Lord Tomorino.

POSEIDON STILL SLEEPS

And when I say, compressed iron, deep down,
Is the substance that makes the Earth expand,
Some say I am a silly circus clown,
And thus should be harried out of the land.
The Continental Drifters hold a barrier,
Leaving no choice except the Trojan horse.
Then I shall challenge and be the torch carrier,
And with new schemes revive another source.
You be the appraiser of the finesse,
As I revamp the time, the place, the scene,
And with full view, be my telling witness:
Meanwhile, I'll portray the difference between

      The endless confusion of the Tower of Babel
      And the quiet wisdom of an Aesop fable.

ODES

(To a Sentimental Celt, Patrick J. Morrissey, Jr., Ph.D.)

Ere ceremonial great fires toppled fresh oaken hearts in
Ireland;
Life came to pass, tested trunks deep in burial turf,
festoons.
Now, mechanical slayers atrophy the useful boggy crypts;
then,
Oaken corpses, uncased, taste fire anew within our
hearths. . .
To Gaelic Greys in Skies or Mood in Lifelong Twilight.
Grey is the top of an aged crow side-sliding in a saved
field;
Grey is the crown of a Mother, who's loved but lost a
reign's place;
Grey is each disappearing evening, ever-dimming coasts;
Grey is each dawn—tomorrow's today's grey. . .
To Our Whiles—Little Winds. . .
A while and death shows us we are not indispensable;
A while and wailing howls foreshadow ominous draughts;
A while, measure for measure, will be one hoary crown;
A while and all you are and have built shall fall quietly
down;
A while and chagrins may well prove Providence's boons. . .
To Memories Many Years Eclipsed. . .
Hot tears scathe cold-flushed cheeks in kinder frustrations;
A snowball squared upon your nose, a fall has hurt you or
pride;
Then, insides glowing from secure senses, embraced by Love;
Yea, hot beverages thaw breathlessness for a calm night—
As fresh falls mat thick thin crusts where we may yet fall. . .

To Fresh-flown Meadows before Tralee Bay. . .
   Blithe spirits twirl in winds, dancing a mystical game. . .
   Beyond stone divides machines mow hay and mice and insect
   hearts.
   A scant shower bathes bodies working or dead in that
   harvest;
   A trumpet sings in the mountain and puffs steam in summer
   sun.
   Silent heralds streak signs amidst that mountainy bosom
   of Kerry.
   Cows low, horses whinny, dogs bark, pigs grunt, fowl
   chortle;
   Women sigh, babies cry, and a fresh pot of tea is made.

THE SAVING GRACE OF MOTHER

"Behold my Mother," said the Son of God,
And the month of May picked up the call.
The flowers and birds and the smile of Nature
All worked together to make transmission clear.

And since that time, in the month of May,
The voice has come rolling down to man
Over the mountains, the vales, and the wastelands,
And heard in cabins, and churches, and castles.

O Mother benign, the world kneels to you.
It loves you, dear Mother, and Love conquers all.
Seize then, thy power of Love over man,
And guide him beside the still waters of peace.

Power over man is in your hands;
You rock the cradle and fashion the child.
You fill the childhood (as is your due)
With truth and love of all mankind.

Often, when storms of hate arise,
And waves of discord rock the nation's barge,
The seed of dutiful motherhood
Will steer our Ship of State to land.

MARTHA

Spirited mother of three
  and grandmother of seven,
Martha brings something free
  to our retirement heaven.

Active at the Natural History Museum
  and Council on International Affairs,
Lively Martha of the Artists' Guild
  helps veterans forget war scares.

To friendly neighbors, not faking,
  five ways she talks with ease
About cooking, gardening, dressmaking
  and more Planned Parenthood activities.

Life is no uninteresting grotto,
  for all who are discerning
May share Martha's marvelous motto:
  "I am still learning!"

SONNET

Enough is said and there is nothing more,
Because it is in knowing that we keep
What forces tremble through us from a deep
That we must but accept and not explore.
And it is best for us that we endure
Until both flesh and soul dissolve in sleep,
At first for one of us, that one may weep
In the slow discipline of being sure.

Between what we may say or ever see,
A vast, expressive silence may arise,
And not a momentary certainty
Torn by the words and phrases we devise;
And yet there is the doubt of what in me
Will justify the challenge of those eyes!

REFUGEE

Dark now and sad the half-light fades
And I, like someone in a wonderland,
Am left beside the sea. The shifting sand,
White from the moon, with awful quiet wades
Into the foam. Long, rolling blades
Of waves assault the shore. Alone I stand
And watch the sea fall short of me, expand,
Lunge back into the darkness where the shades

Of night are drawn. The waves are reaching far,
But I remain secure, America!
Deeper, darker, farther out to sea
The waves splash on and no one hears;
I do not wish to go; there are no tears;
I laugh into the night that I am free!

TUTORED BY HEAVEN

When poverty fades away into the never-never land gone will be its evil strangling hand. Then will humanity rise another notch, and unleash the talents rusted by the world's rain, sleet and slush. Iron bands will bind true love, and break only with the lack of trust. There'll be no cries, no pain, no hypocrites and such as the world will be——Tutored by Heaven and God.

Few will be the lowly souls that will enjoy trampling upon another human being, split and spit the fumes of hell upon innocent lovely scenery. Nobility of mind and nobility of spirit will prevail and find its way into more and more hearts and minds each day. And so, mankind will be lifted once again, by the Grace of God and the——Tutorer of Heaven.

Violation of human rights will cease and at last the world, in dignity and love, will live in peace. No tears will blind people to untruths, no lips, nor sweet mouths, if and when the whole world will stop for one second and listen to the——Tutorer of Heaven.

Then will the honeysuckles sing songs of love and eternal Springs. And as time drops another stormy, violent age, wingless angels to earth will bring life's golden original lessons—lessons taught not by earth but rainbow planets, silvery stars, and the——Tutorer of Heaven.

THE SNOW

White is the snow that falls
Upon the evergreens;

Soon it will cover all
The trees as it leans

Upon the emeralds of Spring,
The amber colors of Fall.

* * *

JUSTICE

Mankind
prides itself
on human justice;

Would that Heavens
thought the same.

Then all the doors
of Heaven,
would be opened;

And none left out
in SHAME!

LITTLE BOY

Little Boy, Little Boy, What do you see?
Gazing out the window so thoughtfully?
Why is the smile upon your face?
Are there fairies about the place
That come to keep you company?
Little Boy, Little Boy, tell me what
You can see that I cannot.

Little Boy, Little Boy, tell me what
You can see that I cannot

* * *

EARTH'S LAMENT

My side lies gouged and bleeding,
My blood is drawn from deep within my veins;
The lymph I built is desecrated
Nor yet comes clean the rain.

My breast is torn for precious fuel
And jagged holes remain.
Deep paths are scarfed across my brow—
How freely have I given.

For pleasures vain, you've destroyed me.
You shall die now.

302

GETHSEMANE

The house is quiet.
I lie awake and pray. . .
'Twas sad news I got today:

"Your child is dying,
Dying, Dear,
Of what just what
We know not."

The house is dark.
I count the time
And hear the solemn church bells chime:

"Your child is dying,
Dying slow,
Of what
We do not know."

* * *

A WORM'S-EYE VIEW

As I go crawling down the street,
I see these folks with just two feet.
The way they rush and hurry on
Soon even those two will be gone.

MONKEY'S VERSION

Three monkeys sat up in a coconut tree,
discussing the issue, said it can't be.
Said one to the other, "Listen, will you?
The rumor being spread, it can't be true;
That humans descended from our noble race,
The very idea—'tis a horrible disgrace.

A monkey would never desert his dear wife,
Quarrel and fight throughout his life.
Nor could it ever be that a mother monk,
would desert her baby. Why, that's the bunk!
Having their babies taken care of by another
till they scarcely would know their own mother!

"There's one other thing you'll never see;
Monkeys building fences 'round a coconut tree.
Think of the coconuts all a-goin' to waste,
Then forbid other monkeys to get a taste.
Why, if I put a fence around that there tree,
Hunger would force the others to steal from me.

"There's one other thing that monkeys don't do:
Stay out all nite, get involved in a stew.
Making whoopee with a gun or a knife;
nor ever take some other monkey's dear life.
We know that man has descended, that orn'ry cuss—
But, brother, he never descended from us!"

C.W. Nelson
A-FISHIN' WE GO

Fishin' season's open, and in a boat we row,
Spring's in the air, so a-fishin' we'll go.
Fish stories tall have always been told;
Fishermen are prone to brag in a manner bold,
We all catch some fish, but this I must say—
Those big ones do always seem to get away.

Some fish will bite eagerly, even on a hook,
While others nibble and just take a shy look.
The bait you use, it may be ever so good.
Well, sittin' too long, you get all pooed.
Finally you get a bite, then what do you say?
Oh, shucks! Smaller then one that got away!

We all know fishermen are prone to exaggerate,
It's just human to say we'll make an estimate.
We've got fishin' equipment; we use every kind;
The place where they bite—it's hard to find.
Now you get a catch after a-fishin' all day;
I'm sorry, my friend, that the big one got away.

The fishermen fret and they make such a stew,
Thinking the fish they caught were all too few.
Well, just throw out your line, wait an' smile;
They'll be right back in a very short while.
Don't let it worry you if one you have in hand,
Is a bit smaller than that one you didn't land.

IN FLANDERS FIELDS

In Flanders Fields flying bombs were heard;
The Allied Armies unto action were stirred.
Cannonballs were fired; the enemy was defied;
While the battle raged on many soldiers died.

In Flanders Field 'side our Allies we fought,
Yea! 't'were honest ideals, the purpose we sought.
While larks in the sky leisurely sing and fly;
The loved ones do mourn o'er those who did die.

In Flanders Fields Allied soldiers had to fight,
Giving their lives for freedom and for right.
Soldiers now live buried where poppies did grow,
With white crosses in silent splendor row on row.

In Flanders Field the gentle breezes now blow,
And white crosses in sunlight beam row after row.
Marking the graves beneath the sod now do lie;
Those, our buddies who in the battle had to die.

In Flanders Fields 'twas where the enemy we fought,
Hoping and praying that the purpose we sought
Would become a reality, in effect at a future time,
When all nations acknowledge God, the ruler Divine.

LOCARNO—1970

We owned Locarno that October morning
As we walked by the Maggiore;

The sky and the water beamed in a Swiss blue
And the distant mountains were veiled by soft clouds.

Cheerfully you fed the swans our breakfast rolls
And I laughed at their haughty indifference to the
            feast;

We touched and talked with our eyes that morning—
And it was no secret that I wanted you.

I caught a glimpse of your face as a mountain
Breeze stirred your hair ever so softly,
And you brushed it gently into place. . .
If only Da Vinci could have painted that moment!

We watched the gaily colored tourist boat puff by
With its Italian flag fluttering,
And you waved a hello. . .

California problems seemed so far away
That morning in Locarno, as our lips touched.

THE MUSIC OF THE UNIVERSE

How often in the stillness of time,
And in the stillness of the night,
Have you heard that universal sound:
The music of the universe?
That all pervading source of
Harmony in all things—
Like a master plan, all things,
Though beset by storms and passions,
Finally unite with the music of the universe
And settle down to a course
That is serene and pervading.

The storm-tossed sea and the elements
Finally settle down to a peaceful course;
The belligerent nations and the angry people—
Their passions surceased—settle
Down to peaceful ways.
They are keyed to the music of the universe,
Of universal harmony and order
That prevail despite all the
Passions, hate, anger, and storms
That best us and our Earth.

TO THE MUSIC OF FREDERICK DELIUS

From the realm of sound

A beauteous mystery weaves

A silver filigree.

In this divine music the world

Becomes transformed,

To blend with mystic,

Sunwashed light.

Magic in the moon and stars—

Sublime in all symphonic glory—

There is no heaven

Which it cannot reach.

JANUARY 15, 1973

Oh, Dr. King, it's your birthday again!
How little we celebrate; how little we have to celebrate;
We commemorate less and less each year.

The bombings continue, Dr. King. And the violence at home.
The Peace work continues, too. And oh, Dr. King, I did
march with the farm workers, and many have stopped eating
Iceberg lettuce, because the farm workers asked us not
to eat Iceberg lettuce, in support of their right to a
union of their choice.

We do think of you, Dr. King, on your birthday!

* * *

AVOCADO TREE, ON A LONELY STREET

Avocado tree on a lonely street—
who could put out such a lovely tree?
What happened, poor avocado tree?
Did they tire of watering you?
Did they tire of moving you so you could reach the sun?
Did they tire of the sight of you?
Did you talk too much, or perhaps not enough?
Did you not like the same T. V. shows as they?
Poor, poor avocado tree, on a lonely street.

* * *

GREEN

Green, oh, where is green? A drop of it, in this asphalt city,
I love. The green is gone, gone with the Spring.
The sky? Would I want it green? Oh, for a drop of
green! Does anybody here have green eyes?

310

MY MOTHER

Many were the years of your toils and your tears,
To bring me thus far to my time of years.
The long winter nights were cold and forlorn;
With the dawn your world became known.
I, as that world, must have caused you great care,
I scampered and hampered all you did there.
My smile was impish when I asked for more bread;
With a very deep sigh you sadly shook your head.
Bringing me up was a bitter-sweet pain;
You knew there would be no rewards to gain.
There is about you a heavenly thing, as sweet as the songs
the morning birds sing.
I watched the brown of your hair turn to silvery gray,
knowing that the love you gave me lit up my way.
How good it was for that babe on your knee; God decided
it should be me.
My love for you can't be measured or told,
It is far too deep and very, very old.

MY MOTHER'S OLD CLOCK

I miss the old homestead that stood in the valley
The timepiece on the mantel running night and day.
Accurate was its timing, and the chime ringing hourly,
On the porch I often heard it where I loved to play.
Its mechanical parts moving was amazing to me
The pendulum slowly swinging made a steady tick-tock;
An old family Bible always lying near it
As the hours passed along on my mother's old clock.

Night creatures during the summertime made familiar sounds;
Bullfrogs beside the mill stream croaked with no fear.
Panther crying in the mountains while roaming around,
The voice of a night owl was frightening and clear.
Mother would tell me a story, then tuck me in bed;
The sound from the pendulum made a steady tick-tock.
Before falling to sleep I heard the chime ringing
As the hours passed along on my mother's old clock.

Many years have gone by since the days of my childhood—
The scenes I remember, containing beauty that I loved:
A range of blue mountains, tall trees in the forest,
And the pleasures God gave as he reigned from above.
I wished I owned the timepiece that stood on the mantel,
And could hear the pendulum swinging make a steady tick-tock
See the wrinkled hand I used to watch wind it
As the hours passed along on my mother's old clock.

ANOTHER DAY

I love the scenes I see at early dawn:
The crystal lake and gracefulness of the swan;
Feel cool morning breezes drifting by;
Marvel at the arc we call the sky;
Hear the roosters crowing on the hill
And the waterfall that's never still;
Cattle in the field begin to stray
I'm thankful, God, to greet another day.

I love the warmness coming from the sun;
Watch the stream of water as it runs;
Eat the fruit that's hanging from the trees
And the honeycomb made by the bees;
See the clouds that form to make the rain
That falls on fields of yellow sugar cane;
Hear my old hound dog begin to bay;
I'm thankful, God, to greet another day.

I love to see the evening sun go down—
The quietness of the night without a sound;
Watch the moon appear up in the sky
And the lonesome planets speeding by;
The Supreme Architect created for you and me
His universe and beauty that we see.
I hope I wake tomorrow and can say,
I'm thankful, God, to greet another day.

COMPLAINING

One winter day I chanced to meet
A crippled beggar on the street;
No sign of sadness on his face
A smile was there to take its place.
I took a pencil from his hand
And dropped a token in his can;
He thanked me twice and was so gay—
But healthy folks complain each day.

Across the street I saw a man,
An old tin cup was in his hand;
On his coat was pinned a sign,
Four simple words, "Please help the blind."
His faithful dog stood by his side
He acted only as his guide;
He smiled as people passed his way—
But healthy folks complain each day.

As I strolled on along the street
I tried to think what makes life sweet:
Its crippled souls who smile at me
Also the blind who cannot see
The sick in pain will always smile—
They fight to live, their life's worthwhile,
In God they trust, each day they pray—
But healthy folks complain each day.

314

AMERICA'S MERCHANT SEAMEN

They man the ships sailing on the ocean,
Through dangerous storms and rolling sea;
Some might not live to see tomorrow,
Or anchor where it's safe to be.
If their life at sea is ended,
And their souls drift with the tide,
May God's angels smile and greet them
When they cross the Great Divide.

* * *

THE LIGHTHOUSE

Standing like a lonely sentinel,
Is the lighthouse by the sea;
Ships and seagulls in the distance,
Make a scene so dear to me.
Nights its beam is always shining,
Through the darkness o'er the bay,
Warning ships and crews of danger
Till the sunlight brings the day.

* * *

MOTHER'S DAY

In the church yard stands a tombstone
At her grave beside the hill;
She is buried 'neath the clover,
Days are lonely, nights are still.
As a child she used to rock me,
Singing songs and always gay;
She is gone but not forgotten,
I honor her each Mother's Day.

315

MY SISTER AND I

Oh, happy childhood, knowing just the sun and joy of life,
Only the singleness of fun, none of the snarls and strife!
The simpleminded, carefree days, exuberant and frank,
With ever-freshened energy and many a harmless prank.

My little sister and I spent our early childhood where
Among the kindly country folk we breathed an unspoiled air,
And came to love the natural things—the grass, the trees,
the hills,
The meadows where the cattle grazed, the little rippling
rills;
We found arbutus trailing low in woods in early spring,
We watched the bare trees bud and bloom, and heard the
robins sing.
We found the violet in the shade half-hidden by its leaves,
And saw the lacy net-like web the wily spider weaves;
The buttercups we picked and held beneath our chins to tell,
By the reflected golden glow, if we liked butter well;
The hoary-headed dandelions we seized in great delight,
And blew the feathery seeds away and watched them out of
sight.

One day, upon an errand bent up to the village store,
I sauntered dreamily along, my thoughts on childish lore;
I crossed the bridge that spanned the creek beside the
blacksmith's place,
When suddenly a barnyard fowl flew right up in my face!
A man who stood nearby rushed up and shooed the bird away;
He said it was a "game cock," so from that eventful day,
Regardless of their harmless look—pastoral, peaceful, tame,
I neared all chickens cautiously, to see if they were "game."

In autumn when the season's dress had glamor in its hue,
When brown and red and yellow flared between the green and
blue,
When mist of early morning melted into golden day,
And fleecy clouds moved o'er the skies and crickets chirped
their lay,
Until the frost that stills and sears fell softly in the
night,
And changed poor Nature's lovely dress from gaiety to blight;
I call to mind how at this time we trudged along to school,
Amid the scents of grapes and pears before the days grew cool.
We passed by gardens rich in yield and fields that groaned
with corn,
To reach the one-room schoolhouse where our study days
were born.

One day a goat came on to school behind a farmer's boy,
This awful presence there for me robbed life of all its
joy;
The bell called all the children in, the goat was left
outside,
He gave a butt against the door then roamed the school
grounds wide;
At recess time he still was there—I stayed indoors in fear,
Then passed the next two hours in dread as our lunchtime
grew near;
At noon the teacher called the goat and, bless her kindly
heart,
Had two boys hold him by the horns—I had a running start.
And that was all I wished as I flew through the village
street;
That afternoon the goat was gone, and life was once more
sweet.

We walked home with the crowd when school was over for the
day,
But bade them all goodbye at length, one couldn't always
play;
We went for milk and raked the leaves and carried water in,
And picked up chips and brought in wood and stacked it in
the bin;
We gathered apples that fell down before their picking time,
And brought them in for sauce and pies, and that was just
sublime;
I took a healthy bite one time into a bright green quince,
I never did repeat that trick; I had a puckered wince.

On winter eves we sat around the kitchen stove and heard
The older folks tell tales of ghosts; we swallowed every
word:
When we were told to go to bed, shudderingly we obeyed,
In shadows of our lamp-lit room the fancied specters played:
Once as I knelt to say my prayers I jumped alert in fright,
I thought I saw an eerie face peek at me from the night;
I bounded lustily down the stairs, my sister at my heel,
I ran to get to older folks who'd know my fears unreal;
Downstairs one adult saw us come and turned about to flee,
This checked my flight and changed my fright into hilarious
glee;
To see a grown-up start to run, not knowing why meanwhile,
Amazed and yet amused me so that to this day I smile.

It took what then seemed endless years to grow and learn
and find
A word that looked disapprovingly on those of simple mind;
Now to regain that child-like mind I seek for help above,
To know the happiness of life, the purity of love.

DO YOU GOT A DOG?

The dusk of evening was stealthily falling,
The hot streets were cleared by the dinner gong;
I trudged impatiently, wearily homeward,
And my woes increased as I went along.

I neared a dooryard and suddenly saw them,
In deep thought and look, an appealing sight;
Two little boys sitting gripped in discussion,
One seemed just past four, the other, not quite.

A break in paving caused walking discomfort,
I stumbled a second, my thoughts a fog;
The woes of childhood were weightless and distant;
Then came, "Hey lady, do you got a dog?"

I paused and thought, "Oh, the quaint little darlings!"
Then answered, "Why yes, I have one. Have you?"
And Just-Past-Four shook his head slowly, sadly,
And the mournful wail of his "Nooo" rang true.

As breaking through sympathic consoling,
Wee Just-Not-Quite-Four, with his face alight,
Piped, "I have one," and his joy was heart-warming,
But his friend, Just-Past, sat in gloom and blight.

I thought again of the woes of young childhood,
The weight became heavy, the distance flew;
"Well, you'll get one," softly I tried to comfort,
As I soberly wound my way anew.

The memory lingered of those little fellows,
As they sat engrossed in their dialogue;
The startling pathos of that plaintive query,
And its "Hey lady, do you got a dog?"

319

Rhoda B. Pierce

AN IDEA

Ethereal, embryonic, illumined,
    It came;
Published and pondered, yet dormant,
    It lurked;
Objectified, patterned, perfected,
    Its fame,
Deep in the hearts of men rooted,
    It worked.

Phillip S. Price

BE THANKFUL

Why should I be Thankful
    When it's so drab outside?
Oh, God's Grace sustains us
    And I know the Sun will rise.

Why should I be Thankful?
    Oh, may I tell you why?
For the goodness in man,
    The beautiful clear blue Sky.

Why should I be Thankful?
    Oh, let me count the ways:
The silence of the nights,
    The brightness of the days.

Shouldn't all be Thankful
    For life and many kind deeds?
The foods that sustain us,
    Yes, the air that we breathe?

YOU

Oh, You are like the Season—Spring—
Spring warms the Earth after Snow and Winter rain;
My Life was all winter till you came,
Touching you, all I could do—love again. . .

Oh, darling, You are my everything—
You have the power to make wild hearts tame;
You make the dormant come to life again;
With you, life is such an exciting game. . .

The warmth of Spring melts the winter snow—
The charm of your smile makes my troubles go. . .
I'm willing for the seed of love to grow,
Oh, I need you—my heart tells me so. . .

WAITING FOR LOVE

A stir in the night!
　Is it you, my Love,
　　is it you?
Come to my arms at last?

Ah!
　T'is but a shadow of
　　dancing flowers
　　high on the garden wall.

I wait.
　And still I watch and wait.

Alas!
　Time is cruel.

* * *

IN MEMORIAM

To those who in the space of time
　have given back their time;

To those who were molded out of dust
　and now are given back to dust;

To those who have lived in honor
　and now have died with honor;

Do we give tribute.

TO STAND ALONE

To Stand Alone. . . .
   My soul a wanton thing,
I stretch my arms as if
   I really flew,
I tried to make my journey's
   flight by wing,
But how could I?
   I was not bird, I knew.

To Stand Alone. . . .
   I journey in the night
As if my eyes were dead
   and I was blind,
And if I had just one
   small lantern light,
I could go on and make
   my journey's find.

To Stand Alone. . . .
   My hand outstretching, to
Clutch the future which
   My soul doth hunger for,
And yet I know not what
   far shore I go,
My senses leaving me,
   I journey o'er.

SUCCESS

Of course discouragement
Must come
When the gamut of life
You choose to run. . .
You must know that
From the start
It takes great courage—
Not a fainting heart. . .
Courage and faith,
The will to win,
Put these together:
Mix love in,
Add compassion,
Some tolerance, too;
This should bring
Success to you.

THE OLD LOG FIREPLACE

The wind blew cold,
The snow piled deep,
But that friendly old fireplace
Made your heart take a leap.

Father read the paper;
Mother mended clothes;
The children did their homework
As the day drew to a close.

No one noticed the cold wind
As it roared outside,
For all was contentment
By the old fireside.

Now we have our shiny stoves
And floor furnaces, too
But the old log fireplace—
They don't take the place of you!

THE DREAMER
(Doctor Martin Luther King)

The dreamer had a dream that gave
Thought, much to ideas and ideals!
The kind that expressed how
Many true and loyal citizens feel;
A dream that challenged young
And old American Negroes' democracy.
The dreamer was brave, true,
Kind, loving and non-violent;
He never knew the word hypocrisy;
His only desire was to help humanity.
Regardless of what the cost might be
The dreamer knew his fellow man's needs.
But the fate of the dreamer was a tragic plight,
All because of prejudice, you see,
Hatred, bigotry, malice and greed;
So one day he fell by the way.
Yes, he fell in a wise, merciful,
And loving Savior's care.
Farewell to the dear dreamer,
Yet the precious, realistic dream,
Was instilled in the hearts of youth,
And the hearts of countrymen;
The dream will be cherished to the end.
Farewell, to the dreamer, farewell!
The dreamer had a dream!

MY MOM, THE PRINCESS

I'm Pearl Astrona, whom you may have read of
In Mom's book of poetry *NO LONGER DEFEATED
AND OTHER POEMS,*
Intrinsically combined with her many virtues, nature and love.
Yes, I'm she, her little bundle of joy, whom she lovingly
speaks of.

How fortunate I am that she did not wait longer;
For who knows, had she, I might have been somewhere yonder.
Yes, I'm she, that good and lovable little girl,
Affectionately known to everyone by my name: PEARL.

Mom's love and loyalty will everlastingly live in my heart;
A helping hand with stimulating confidence was her part.
My Grandma, bless her! with my aunts kept careful check
upon the rein;
As they taught me to be free of prejudice, and hate never
to maintain.

Grown now and with a family of my own;
How well I've learned, and also prone
To know that being a career girl, mother, and wife,
Is not an easy task for any woman in this life.

My Mom has done it and succeeded well;
She's my darling, and to her grands she's swell!
Loved by all she takes the cake,
For she's down to earth; she's not deceptive and nothing
about her is fake.

(Written by PEARL ASTRONA QUINTYNE for her
mother.)

SUNRISE

If you have looked into the East
    To see the rising sun,
You gazed upon a sight supreme—
    Another day begun!
And this symbolic splendor
    Of Love, new Light, new Hope,
Can keep you thru your darkest hour—
    No matter what the scope.
The clouds of darkness cannot stay—
    THE SUN MUST RISE AGAIN!
And with it springs a bright new day—
    God's perfect Love! Who can explain?

* * *

YESTERDAY, TODAY AND FOREVER

I cannot doubt that Jesus lives
    The same as yesterday,
Nor can I doubt He cares for me
    In a very personal way.
For recently his presence came
    With glorious warmth untold—
A fellowship so wonderful
    That I did not behold
Till later on, that while we supp'd
    Together, Christ and I,
His Pow'r had healed me, just like those
    He touched in days gone by.

DIFFERENCE?

There was a time "back when,"
    There was a time, O yes.
People sang and danced then;
    They also lived and loved then;
They are gone now, aren't they?
    Or have they been set aside?
Or is this a continuation of that
    which has gone before—or what?
There is a time now,
    A different time now, O yes.
People still sing and dance;
    They also live and love;
They perform "the miracle" as well.
    There was a time, there is a time.
Listen to the old song, listen to the new,
    Think of old love, think of love now.
Was there any more then? Is there any less now?

LATE TO BLOOM

We planted a rose bush
                    three years ago.
It survived, greened and budded;
                    it didn't grow.
Winter took its will away;
                    anyone should know
Jack Frost doesn't play favorites
                    in winter's throe.
In our naiveté we languished;
                    it didn't grow.
Spring came, then went again;
                    did we know?
The plant we planted abstained;
                    it didn't grow.
November came round, not harsh,
                    IT blossomed, Ho!

* * *

TIME (THE HEALER)

I'd give the world to see her—would I were
invited to. . .
Yet I hesitate to impose myself upon the
other two. . .
The other two are she and she, as by all means
ought be. . .
They dwelt together and stay as one in exclusion
as we. . .
If time would heal a wound or two so that we may
but see. . .
No gap too wide to separate us, she and she
and we. . .
Then it could truly claim the title that has been bestowed
on it.

331

A CHRISTMAS PRAYER

As we prepare to celebrate
Our Dear Saviour's birth,
I hope mankind will accept   •
And bring peace to this earth.

Man, almost from creation,
Has taken from God's land,
Without giving anything back
To help his fellow man.

Too long man has lingered
With his war and pain.
History has shown us
We all must refrain.

Jesus came with peace and love,
His gift to every man.
How long can we go on
Before we understand?

On this Christmas Eve,
As the Star of David shines,
I pray that love and peace
Will be our biggest find.

EXPANDED

A rose exploded in morning light;
The dawn sends a lover who waits for me.
A tree sends a leaf down to lazily light
Upon shattered sidewalks leading out to the sea.

Oh, seashore, smash me out a melody;
Who will walk with me to my infinity?
Seashore, take my herd and take my land,
There's patience in my lover's hand;
All other ground is desert sand.

Oh, wind that leads clouds around,
Show me my lover. Where's she found?
O, sunshine, glow on my lover's head,
Making my lover's face to show.
Wind that levels mountains, roaring down,
Take my woven pieces away to you.
Lead high above without a sound;
When my lover comes, I won't know what to do.

* * *

VOTER'S REQUIEM

Who will pay the price for your freedom?
Who will take your life and let you lead it?
Sit and watch as the money starts.
Your mind slips away.
Smile as you elect your leader.
His money rules the way 'til your dying day.

LUNCH INTERLUDE

It was today I saw a friend
I hadn't seen for long, so long.
Then I heard my gay heart sing
A welcoming and a joyous song.

For I thought often of this one,
And wondered why we had not met,
Tho' I walked the selfsame paths
We once had trod in sunny gold or rainy wet.

When now I look into those eyes,
Receive an answering friendship glance,
Then I realize that happy eyes,
As happy feet, may gaily dance.

We talk of this and speak of that,
What whosit did, where's what's-her-name?
Still like your job and what you do?
And so we play the mundane game.

Perhaps it is a silly game
And we say things that don't mean much,
But friendship needs no certain words
Nor any special feel or touch.

It's really quite enough to know
That we may meet again sometime,
In between, somewhere, somehow,
One of your moments will be mine.

Thus, looking, laughing, happy, we
Forget the time passing so fast.
We think not of the words we say
But try to make each moment last.

How long are thirty minutes, then,
A lifetime, or a moment, friend?

* * *

BEAUTY NAP

The lady sleeps.
Even though it's not her usual bed
That greets her slumber,
She sleeps now.
How rests she, then,
On that pillow of steely metal bred
Which backs her seat
Within the City bus?

She's no less beauty,
As from Morpheus' cup this one sips,
Than she who waited
Prince's kiss.
And I would,
Yet must not touch hers with these lips,
And wake her from that
Moment's bliss.

MOOD FOR FROLIC

Not today are my thoughts like a city,
        rectangular, numbered, and groaning beneath the hand
of man; I am a part of earth, witty
        of meanings unspoken, or a tree I stand
with quivering leaves, or water which plays with the sun
and casts on high its broken lights. Run
with me, be a sunset, be a windtossed one.

* * *

MOON DREAMS

In ghostly, serried line,
        a ragged tree-troop climbs the moonward way,
        but stands before a hill fence in dismay.
And Mister Moon looks down, benign,
and casts a dreamy silver-shine
athwart the valley, mist-enshrined.

* * *

SOLEMNITY

O Happiness, importunate,
        that calls to me across the years,
you are the subtle distillate
        of sweetly bitter brews of tears
that murmur in life's samovar.
        You are not thralled by human craft;
we cannot lure your fragrance far
        unless we drink the sober draft—
        the sweetly bitter brews of tears
that murmur in life's samovar.

COINS OF LOVE

If somewhere along the way
You meet
Begging, a little famished one,
Warm him with your loving smile.
Have pity—compassion;
Tender a light caress.

Don't be deceived by appearances;
Perhaps the pain of his
child years of hunger,
etched in the little face,
Is only the symbol
Of his real, great need.

Begging for so little—"Love."

* * *

IDENTITY

You bring with you
My disposition—
At times, shining light—
At times, total darkness—

THE TREE OF LIFE

The tree of life grows strange, 'tis true,
   Its roots compose the basic you.
The tiny sprout that seeks its way
   Finds new adventure every day.
A straight young sapling reaches high,
   As free from care as birds that fly.
Maturity brings branches new,
   Each one a challenge you've come through.
As branches split and spread out wide
   Love and experience flourish inside.
The full-grown tree is straight and tall,
   Showering radiance over all.
The leaves are trophies you have won
   For all the good things you have done.
Those little sprouts that cluster 'round,
   Represent new life you found,
As tired old trees must wither and die,
   So, my friend, must you and I.

* * *

THE FIREPLACE

The logs in the fire
   Burn out.
The ash glows red,
   The embers crumble.
Tendrils of smoke
   Curl up the chimney.
Lingering on the hearth,
   A fragrance of yesterdays.

338

SEASONAL LADY

She flew so quickly through the door,
All windy twirls and gay,
With lips so crisp and berry-red
She bade me a good day.

She smiled and cool things came to mind
Like breezes, brooks, and rain;
Her presence seemed to fill me
With a very sad refrain.

The register was there to sign
And with a blue-white hand,
She took the pen and signed her name
With letters, swift and grand.

A cloche of green and yellow leaves
Caressed her rich brown hair;
A scarlet scarf embraced her neck
And crackled in the air.

Sonatas seemed to fill the room
With sounds so glorified,
A melancholy surge took hold
From somewhere deep inside.

Her blazing dress of orange seemed
A slice of early dawn;
Her burnished coat cast forth a gleam
Like gold and yellow corn.

Her rustic scent was fresh and clear
Like green grass kissed by dew;
It brought to mind a forest scene
Of red and golden hue.

"My bags will come this afternoon,"
She smiled so mystically.
"Your room," I said, "is down the hall,"
And handed her the key.

I looked into her chestnut eyes
And asked how long she'd stay.
"Three months," she said, with twinkled brow,
And briskly walked away.

I waited till I heard her steps
Grow light, then disappear,
And reaching for the register
I quickly brought it near.

Her name was there, so bold and free,
In letters, large and small;
I said it soft and then aloud:
She wrote, "Miss Autumn Fall."

SHARON'S PRAYER

Dear Lord, what language do You speak?
Do You know what I'm saying in Polish, Irish, or Greek?
Do You hear us, Your children of Italy and Nice
When we beg in all languages for that long-sought peace?

Dear Lord, what color is Your skin?
Do You care what mine is, or do You care what's within?
Do You care where I originate, which wordly part,
Or do You judge me by the goodness in my heart?

Dear Lord, please let me see Your gentle face,
So that we, Your children, will know the Superior Race—
Or is there a reason for this mystery so vast,
That has puzzled mankind from generations past?

Dear Lord, an inner voice tells me I will find
Together, with all humanity, the sighted and the blind,
On the Day of Judgment, we of the human race,
Will be hearing Your voice and will then see Your face.

MAN VS. GOD

An unceasing losing battle is waged by Man,
Hopelessly challenging God in every way he can—
In perpetual competition, he stumbles and gropes,
Striving to top Him, achieving his fondest hopes.

"I've created a tree to match Your own,
A grass so green, the greenest I've ever known."
"But can it blossom in Spring, shed its leaves in the Fall?
Does it shelter the birds that sing and call?
Does your grass have roots to nourish and feed?
Can you feel the dew? does it grow from seed?"

"I've created a rose and many beautiful flowers,
Utilizing my talents and oh, such tedious hours!"
"But can it bloom from a bud and open its eyes,
Each petal revealing a magnificent surprise?
Is the fragrance like nothing else on this earth
As it unfolds its beauty, its miraculous birth?"

"I've probed outer space but I didn't see You;
Your angels and saints were nowhere in view."
"Who do you think blazed your trail,
Making your moon trips successful, without fail?
You felt My presence, to Me you prayed—
I gave you courage, you were never afraid.
The 'fireflies' you saw were wondrous indeed—
It was My path of stardust to help you succeed."

Man may be a genius with a brilliant mind,
But creating his brain is God's work—one of a kind.

GOD'S LITTLE CHILDREN

God created His children in various shapes,
And colored their skins with beautiful shades.
Spoke He: "Love one another, as I love ye all,
For ye are my children, and are brethren to all."

The black child's life was filled with woes,
The brown child's land was taken by foes,
The yellow child's cunning could not be trusted,
And the white child, feeling superior, strutted.

Why should the color of a brother's skin matter,
As long as his heart is warm and tender?
Why judge another by the shape of his eyes,
When what's in them should be judged by the wise?

Why do we condemn the religions of others,
When they, too, practice the teachings of Father's?
Love one another, for we are all brethren,
And someday we'll meet our Father in heaven.

ASTRAL TRIP

I rested one afternoon on a warm, lazy day,
And drifted to slumberland, dreaming all the way.
I saw my body rise and float away somewhere,
While chimes of silv'ry bells echoed in the air.
Looking around drowsily, "Where's this?" I mused aloud,
And found that I was riding on a white, fluffy cloud.
The scenery was lovely, like a Disney fairyland,
And in the distant shore surf rolled on the sand.

A little angel passed by, playing on his harp,
His golden wings were spread like a flying carp.
I stared in fascination; could this be paradise?
Is this what happens to a soul when his body dies?
Suddenly my senses reeled, I fell without a sound;
Like a tiny falling star, I was homeward bound.
Looking down I got a shock—my body slept below!
With a white flash we fused, and I woke from the glow.

Two more astral trips I took when I lay asleep;
One was to a mountaintop, where I tended sheep;
The other was a desert, brightly lit at night
By stars that were diamonds; what a wondrous sight!
What *really* happens to our souls when our bodies die?
Do they go on astral trips and float up in the sky?
If the places I have seen were glimpses of Eden,
I pray that my soul may live someday in heaven.

Virgie McCoy Sammons

MY FRIEND

My friend is someone

To whom I can come

When I'm joyful or sad,

To share either, and make glad.

One who is sincere,

Who is pleased to be near;

One who to one's self is true,

Who believes I'm that, too.

One whose thoughts mingle with mine,

Touching the low, and heights divine;

A friend so true is never denied;

Two minds, two souls confide.

SCATTER KINDNESS

Scatter kindness here and there,

Lift a spirit, dry a tear;

Give a smile along life's way,

A bit of joy in what you say.

Share with the lonely beauties free,

Light a candle that the blind may see;

Give to others what God gives to thee:

Love, compassion and serenity.

* * *

WHO CAN TOUCH A BREEZE?

Who can touch a breeze

When it passes through pine trees?

We know it's there by trembling leaves,

For that is all one really sees.

346

Virgie McCoy Sammons

Who can touch a thought

An awakened conscious brought,

To bring the heart to sing

Of beauty, and love and things?

Who can touch the color

Of morning's sunrise red?

Or imagine another

More beautiful instead?

Who can touch the light

Of moon and stars at night?

Or touch the reason why

Flowers lift their faces to the sky?

These things are too divine to touch;

That's why we care so much.

But who would dare to touch?

For to touch would tarnish such.

A PRAYER FOR PEACE

O, dear Lord, let there be peace
On earth, in the homes, and in the streets.
Let there always be a smile,
A friend, and a hug.
Do not abandon us in time of need,
For there's nothing worse than a broken heart.

* * *

LOVE

Love is smiles, joy, happiness.
Life is.
Love is cries, screams, hatred.
Death is.
Love is whatever you make it.

* * *

A THOUGHT

In the quiet of the night
When no sound can be heard,
All is still as if dead—
Dead as if for a hundred years.
A thought lingers in the mind;
Memory lane's delight
Of bygone days of yesteryear
Seen in a flash of an eye:
A picture of a past being born.

BEFORE THE SUN

Walk the winter beach alone
At dawn and feel the cold grey stone—
Grindings of a million years
Beneath your feet.

Long-dead tree branch and root seaborne,
Scoured satin, oyster-white, forlorn,
At last lie worn, at rest
Against the dune.

Gray chiffon fog billows in
To veil the silver sea within
Its moist and secret shroud, in haste,
Before the sun.

Drab sea birds break the lowering sky;
Dun-colored wings and shrieking cry
In ancient ritual to greet
The morning light.

Walk the winter morning beach
And find serenity to reach
Deep in your soul—courage to face
The bright brass day.

MOMENTUM

Peaceful, placid, still and deep;
To the unwary it seems to sleep.
Mirrowing trees along its edge—
When did the change come?

So gradual, no one noticed the
                    waters twirl and spin,
Gaining speed as they gaily beckon all
                    to follow the mountain path,
Strewn with rocks and impending danger.

Hurrying, splashing, whirling,
Inviting, tempting, teasing, taunting;
Too late: tearing, beating, crashing,
                    crushing;
Leaving havoc in its wake.

* * *

SOLILOQUY

"Why did I stand so mute?" Silence
            made me seem cold. My heart
was hurting so. "Oh Lord!"
            My son lay so still and white,
as I waited beside his bed
in the Intensive Care ward.
            No sign was there that said
he knew I was with him.
Till one day as I watched so closely
            A tear slid from beneath his eyelid,
and the chills rolled over me.
            I told him of his twin,
Of his daddy, too; in fact,
All his family and friends praying for him.

350

SONNET FOR A SUNDAY NIGHT

We walked along the city streets at night
Beneath half-hearted tries of drizzly rain.
Philosophy and poetry we used as light
To guide our paths, in hope of spirits' gain
In things esthetical. Did we decide
The universe to be a hollow ball,
And people creatures crawling in the dark inside?
Did we decide the universe was ALL?
I took your hand and both of us kept talking.
The rain fell slightly faster through the dark,
The street felt less deserted for our walking,
And then we found a bench inside the park.
Who knows how the way of this world goes?
What's most important is a single rose.

GENESIS 1:1-26, 3:17-19

A molten mass of burning gas
Was flung in ever-widening gyre
And formed a ball, when time did pass,
Out of a cataclysmic fire.

And from this ball large chunks were thrown
That cooled and turned to spheres of rock.
Nine gods were giv'n their crown and throne,
And Life upon one orbit knock'd.

The Ruler granted it should stay;
Life thanked Him, then turned to the sea,
And filled it with a grand array
Of creatures that one could not see.

Then He turned slowly to the land,
And seeing nought but hard cold rock,
Created soil and grass and sand,
So walking fish could learn to walk.

Next, Life put creatures on the soil;
A little later He made Man
Who, if he cares to live, must toil
And make the earth yield all it can.

This is the way that it all began:
        How, my friend, will it end?
This is the way it all began
From nothing to the time of Man.
        How, my friend, will it end?

THIS RIVER OF MIND

Into which infinity of wasteless time
Brings this being they call mine?
Is it a spring in the universe,
Shooting ripples of water and bubbles to burst?

Is it the limb of the tallest oak tree,
Stretching far into the warm sun,
Daring mere mortals to set me free,
Or question the life from which I begun?

Oh, I know they search for me,
And probe into the resources of my mind,
This physical shell of me,
And whatever else they hope to find.

But I would suggest they walk by the river's bank,
Warmed by the closing sun,
Where God recognizes no mortal's rank,
Alone by the work he has done.

I would suggest, like the tallest oak tree,
They reach into the sky
To find the spirit,
The spirit that is I.

Or maybe in the spring where the cool waters flow,
There they will find my soul,
There they will hear my spirit ring,
"I know! I know!"

And by the river's bank where its waters run free,
Where mortals say there are two of me,
It is them I ask, of the river you see,
"How many riverlets in thee?"

There are many, many, you see,
That make up the river to be,
This river, this spirit that is me,
This oak tree that longs to be free
In a universe—a part of me.

My fellow mortals, I remind you to be
Ever so very careful in your search of me,
For it is in God my liberty will be,
To let me—I pray—be only me.

MY MOTHER

Your praises by the world remain unsung,
Yet to me no praise I have can overestimate
The kind deeds you did, the mercies shown among
Your little world of neighbors in and out your gate.

There was a halo always in your smile,
An inner light that round you beamed,
A kindly welcome always on your doormat, while
All who crossed caught your radiance, it seemed.

A friend to all—a loving wife—a blessed mother—
To the world these phrases may simple be;
In lovelier words poets sing of many another,
But these spell NOBLE, GREAT and GRAND to me!

* * *

EASTER AND SPRING

Easter and Spring!
Why shouldn't we sing?
For immortality to the earth they bring.
The one, Holy for our Lord should be;
The other, happy that the world may see
The Power and the Glory of the resurrection morn,
Truth and beauty of all nature in every soul reborn!

SONNET TO NATURE'S BEAUTY

Abundant beauty ever greets the eye
Throughout the length of this wondrous domain,
As one looks eastward to a fertile plain
From crest of Ouachita or Ozark high.
Here tiny rivulets from shady vales
Join arms to form the winding, bubbling brooks
That tarry at the cool, secluded nooks,
Then, laughing, dash through narrow verdant dales.
Let not a vast industrial inroad
With its wanton waste be made here afresh,
With lavish profits chiefly as its goal;
Guard well what Mother Nature has bestowed.
While fortunes may pamper and feed the flesh,
It is nature's beauty that feeds the soul.

* * *

SONNET ON THE FATE OF VENICE

O beauteous city!! In the days of yore
Your commerce excelled that of any land.
Rich-laden vessels came from distant shore
To bargain with the merchants of your strand.
The arts with splendor by your wealth was bought:
Grand edifices of marble and stone,
Works which Titian and Bellini wrought,
Other masters among the best e'er known.
Travesty! Selfish, vain cupidity
Caused man to build you on those mounds of clay.
The acid fumes from his technology
Erode the marble, make the art decay.
'Tis symbolic of what man's fate will be
As you sink in the mire beneath the sea.

356

SONNET

Time for work and time for play,
Sing and walk for time this day.
Laughter if you want it, and sobs if you care,
But always have time if you must dare.
Time, you may sure, is twenty-four hours
You can plant some lovely flowers.
Time is the measure of kites and kings,
Minutes and seconds and hours have wings.
Poems may write and novels revise;
Time for dreams, times for wise.
Choose paints stand out the easel's palette;
Those who wish for printers' etiquette
Stand up and fight or watch the dogs bay;
This time someone has to weigh.

* * *

PRETTY BOYS

I think that I shall never see
Such boys can use to see
Girls can laugh and play and sing,
But boys must work and do their thing.

THE CRY OF THE AGNOSTIC
"Help Thou my unbelief"

My tears are blinding and I am so lost
In the universal globe on which I live,
And in which my decay will remain, when
death claims this person I.
I wonder what will spring forth from my
waste. Will it be flowers? plants? worms?
Other animals must feed from me
So human man can survive from them.
And why will he be here to travel again
the road I trod?

Oh, my tears are blinding and I am so lost,
For there is nothing everlasting to cling to.
How I wish there was a God so I could humbly
pray for understanding of this earth,
And why, oh why, I am here.
If only I, as others do, could believe in
simple faith,
I'd kneel tonight and plead to God, the
Most High, to give knowledge that belongs
with the mind.
Oh, what is a brain? A useless thing
When I know nothing of my Maker and my life's
course.

My tears are blinding; I can hardly see.
Oh, pray tomorrow may still set me free,
free from thoughts happier beings do not
have.
And yet to be thus, with no thirst to know,
I'd rather cease to be at all.
Then heaven, heaven help me, what am I?
Must I just live, just die, that others may
still live so they may die?

358

My mind doubts the existing God,
Eternity everlasting to cling to, O Lord!
Perhaps men in generations to be
Will find a purpose for the birth of Me!

* * *

CRUEL BLOW OF LOVE

All of a sudden the world has changed;
It's empty, gloomy and dismal again.
Oh, what is life that it has to be
So heartless and so cruel to me?

Perhaps I know and understand too well
The pitiful expressions and emotions of man.
I see too well, I feel too deep,
I understand and think, think—not sleep.

Into the man's mind I gazed
And, oh behold, he was half-crazed.
Guilt beat upon his tortured heart,
blameing him needlessly, but he could not see.
Oh, what, what, about me?
What about me? I cried.

Then in the silence of my soul I knew,
Knew it was he—he, not me.
I'd lead the way for him to go,
To find ease, comfort, and perhaps love to know.
Peace was not for him while worries, doubts,
confused his soul;
Even his emotions were out of control.
This was not a time to think of me, no, no,
It was he—he, not me!

I picked a time when my emotions would not show
and I struck the one hopeful blow!
Sympathy had been given long enough, understanding
far too much, and yet he cried, he cried!
I struck the one cruel blow;
Why? He'd never know.
One cruel blow to make him think; to stir the emotions;
make him bitter; make him angry; make him grow!
To fight back, to climb back up—up over the borderline!

I succeeded! It was the only way,
The cruel blow of love, cruel because of love.
He would never know. He would hate me but I
would be kind.
Kind, never letting him know that when his feelings
of kindness changed toward me it was because of
my love for him,
For, knowing this would happen, I could not stand by
when he was in need of the cruel blow, the cruel blow
of love!

The world will change again for someone, somewhere, and
again I will see too well, feel too deep, understand and
think, think—not sleep.
How to help, what to do! God will again see me through.

Perhaps when I am in need, someone will love enough to strike
the one cruel blow of Love to help me.
Probably I will not understand that this is love.
Until it is I or someone else, God, let me be happy again.

DEATH WAIT

If you should die and I should live
My death would be worse than yours.
Who knows how long the years might be
that I must struggle on?
With tears and strife I'd live a life
Worse than the death of yours.

Few ever know the height we reached;
Few ever feel the depth so deep;
Two minds, two bodies, two souls so
complete.
That even through death they will feel
and meet.

And in the silence of the darken nights,
Grief and tears embedded so deep within
my soul
Will call you back to me,
Until I feel your nearness and laugh
triumphantly over death.

Reminiscences of happiness and sorrow
That so combined our life on earth with
eternal love,
Will keep you close beside me through all
my days.
Awakening memories which will never sleep
Shall guide my living death to yours.

And only death can reach the dark and dreadful
grief
Which will lie deep in the recesses of my mind
and claim the senses;
And will no longer know that you are gone;
And only then will my death be less than yours.

Ruth R. Shepherd

EMANUEL

A Leader was born;

His cradle was made of weeds and clay,

His initials were LBJ.

He grew by leaps and bounds,

The Americans learned from him and they trusted.

He was a symbol of Moses and the bulrush.

The Bible tells me (and I hold these words to be true), that the number of people in the beautiful garden was only two.

Adam and Eve were the parents of creation and that's true;

If they were your parents, they were my relations, too.

Man was made from the dust of the earth, and to dust he must return to the ground.

It made no difference if the face of our leader was white and the face of his fellow American was brown.

So that awful day in Dallas, when the reins were left in his hand, he mounted the wings of an Eagle made by man.

America was just recovering from a case of high blood pressure creed, and the chart showed a decline of anemia for need.

He chose for his running mate a man he loved a lot.

The change was not easy, but he was a chip off the solid rock.

And with the trust and obedience of the Democratic Party was
the old standing block.

They challenged Civil Rights and no President had worked so
hard for,

And with a stroke of a pen he signed many of them into law.

None of us came here to stay, but I'm glad I lived in the
time he passed this way.

They buried him near the River Pedernales.

But he is not alone, for the shade of the old oak and his
work under the Lone Star will always tell.

And millions and millions of Americans will pass and say;
Here lies. . . .

EMANUEL!

SUSPENSE

I listen to the talking, talking,
I hear the restless walking, walking.
Oh, dear God, will You please
Put his tortured mind at ease?

He's waiting for that phone to ring,
No matter what the call does bring.
Any news is better than none,
Just so this talking, walking is done.

Alas, the ring, not too soon;
Hurried steps across the room.
Quiet murmurs across the miles,
Is the silence just a guile?

And now there is a running, running,
Like a hunter gunning, gunning;
Down the stairs and to my room,
The talking, talking is resumed.

But this time the voice is clear,
The countenance devoid of fear.
On his cheeks the tears do glisten;
With relief, I sit and listen.

METAMORPHOSIS ON BIRTH

Dusk, all pale, awaits her maturity,
    Gently swaying within the arms of Day;
Night softly calls her to his obscurity—
    He models Dawn from her sleeping clay.

* * *

TRIOLET

The tulip guards the daffodil
    And scares the furred mole away.
It is by kind Nature's will
The tulip guards the daffodil.
Planted low or on a hill,
    Side by side, night or day,
The tulip guards the daffodil
    And scares the furred mole away.

* * *

REQUIEM TO SUMMER

Wistful Autumn with your soft rains blowing,
Damp with weeping is your grass yet green.
Tearful you cry "Summer is going. . ."
Her faded dress is still to be seen.
Over the meadows the trees bow in silence,
Waving a moanful—a sweet goodbye.
Maple leaves blinking, and they are winking:
"She'll come again, she'll dress again
In colors of old rainbow splendor;
Kissing again, embracing again
Like lovers that kiss through their tears."

TO THE LADIES

I wish I was a cotton ball
So very white and fluff—
So on your dresser I could lie
And be your powder puff.

But why do I such things aspire?
These things could never be,
For I would see a lot of things
Not meant for me to see.

* * *

AN AUTHOR—HIS WORK, HIS DREAM

The clouds, like ships, sail a sea of blue,
Inviting me to leave a writer's task
And charter space to some land and do
The things I would, without the need to ask
Is what I wish to write, right or wrong,
Or just my dream to be carefree all day long?

Reinold Shubert

TO A YOUNG LADY

I found a large sea shell on the beach—
Would I hear a hum, a whisper, or words to
teach?
Perhaps kind words of cheer, hope or
sorrow. . .
I could only hear; "Do your work today, not
tomorrow."

I know you, too, as a fair young maiden
Has heard the shells whisper, a Prayer on
Wings. . .
In your daily chores, light or heavy-laden,
Practice to be faithful in little things.

WHEN YOU LEAVE THIS WORLD

When you leave God's troubled world
   Is there any reward you can expect?
Will they miss you when you're gone?
   While here, what did your life reflect?

When you leave God's troubled world,
   When life on this earth you depart,
Can they say anything good about you?
   Could they say "He had a good heart?"

When you leave God's troubled world
   And your whole life here is spent,
Will they view, at length, your remains,
   And wonder which place you went?

When you leave God's troubled world
   And news of your departure they tell,
Will those who knew you quickly decide
   Whether you went to Heaven or to Hell?

What will they say on your tombstone?
Just that you lived, and here you rest?
Will that just about cover everything,
   Or did you bring to earth any happiness?

Paul Sights

OLD FOLKS

When we get old and we are quite feeble,
  With no teeth and with hair almost white,
We are filled with pain in the daytime
  And there's no rest for us at night.

Folks will tell us how much they love us;
  They're nice, want to make us feel good,
But we know they'd like to get rid of us
  If there was some sly way they could.

Why are there so many of us old people?
  Why on this earth do we have to stay?
When it seems we serve no good purpose
  And it's better in Heaven, so they say.

The flowers, the grass, the vegetables—
  They die, but live anew with the seasons
But old Man, he just lives on and on,
  And it seems for just no good reason.

But it must be in God Almighty's plan
  That old people stay around till He calls.
Anyway, they can do nothing about it—
They'll just have to wait, that's all.

BIRTH, DEATH, INFINITY

Birth, death, infinity
Another holy trinity. . .
From cradle to grave,
for eternity we crave,
for the answers in every vicinity. . .
The sun bids us welcome,
the moon bids adieu,
It casts its grandeur upon me and you.
And in this esthetic contemplation,
I feel that I'm in love with the universe,
but dwarfed by its majesty; yet
through the peripheral
vision of my soul,
I discovered a new dimension.
Infinity, Eternity, and a new Serenity,
and life could never be the same.

* * *

ECSTASY REBORN

The dawn had broken.
The heavens again opened their eyes to the
                tomorrow of yesterday.
Just as the darkness diminishes me
The dawn enlarges the spectrum of my soul,
And I find that I am trapped
By the inner surges of a power greater than life.

Dawn comes as a majestic crown,
                glorifying earth.

Olivia S. Snead

ODE TO MY LOVE

I yearn for you, my love;
Now, in the stillness of this quiet day,
I think of you and the beauty that is you;
I see you in my mind's eye
The last time I saw you,
Just a few hours ago—
And the joy and love which filled me at the
                sight of you
Is with me still.

I wonder and I weep
At the tears and pain
        I caused you;
The sweetness of you
Fills my entire being,
And the love I have is so great
I cannot help but wish
That we could live that time again—
And I would give you the joy and love
You have always needed,
And so many times I have kept from you.

My love, forgive me for those painful times—
If you could but say the words
Of forgiveness and love,
My heart would leap with happiness.

I pray to God that you will
Never be lost to me;
I pray that I be given the ability
To bring you happiness.

Forever shall I love you—
Forever need you—
And every day I shall strive
To bring you joy, peace,
And everlasting love.

VARIABLES

Sometimes I think
My house is tall:
High noon of summer—
Ambition gazes at the stars;
Flattery praises my desires.
    Vanity, coveting applause,
        Cloys the truth,
        Betokens fall.

And then again
My house is small:
Weatherbound—
Gossip freezes the tender heart;
Envy squeezes the spirit poor.
    Doubt, divorcing logic,
        Shrivels the heart,
        Divines the depth of fall.

Sometimes I have
No house at all:
Weather begs description—
Inconstancy unseats intention;
Penury defeats repose.
    Dullness, lacking challenge,
        nullifies existence,
        Obscures the fall.

Sue Snorf

PURSUIT

From a dome of twilight
the barn-swallow emerges—
practiced boomerang in flight—
banking
sky-diving
skimming gracefully
miniature sea gull of the skyway.
A sharp, quick cry
and roger
banking
diving
swiftly, accurately,
unerring dart—
the swallow feeds
in flight.

SISTER AGNES

I have need of the night,
But find it made brittle
By moon satellite. . .

I have need of the sun,
But find it obscured
By the veil of a nun. . .

* * *

MILKWEED POD

Miser's purse
grows round and full,
till the thief
of autumn steals
from wrinkled age
its hoard
and, tripping on the wind,
spills its treasure—
fulfilling
Nature's immutable law.

* * *

MISTY WOODS

Wings of silver gauze,
swirling about silver beeches
with silver lichens
vanish,
like silver frost,
in an opalescent morning.

FLAME THROWER

October arsonist
flung a torch of triple-plated marigolds
onto hillside woods;
hurled a blaze of scarlet sage
among spurious thickets and trailing ivy;
tossed a flare of bronzed mums
and stain of purple asters
into beech woods,
then watched the rioting dyes
ignite a crimson bonfire in western skies. . .

Having burned the loveliness of summer
in effigy
the flame-thrower,
exhausted by his revelry,
reeled into monochrome November
with only burned-out embers
of his gaudy show. . .

LIGHT POEM

I see the light
And it shines beyond my sight. . .
My fear is persistent
that it shall not stream
its most marriageable human beam
to my own most essential sight, insistent.

And what do I see?
The common sift of stream I see of it,
Enfolding me partially in a golden dream,
I now encrouch its race on me
When it endows its face of splendency
             in the Night's fit. . .

* * *

GOODBYE

I sought the day when my heart was may
I sought the noon hours in their bequeathing
And the miasma of the murmuring months
Brought silver in their sheathing.

The anemone was now
The radiance was worthy
Of more light to the transfixed translator
O to the courage of merry, bursting summers

The bees to their clanging nectar
Forestall the shivering grief on the branch:
The hive of heaven is now portal to: adieu.

IN MEMORIAM

A new dawn broke over Camp Tomahadge
Its campers in a restless slumber,
Dreaming of plots and pranks to hatch
Inspiring to sports a great number.

Finally the bugle sounded reveille,
Willing or not, all had to rise,
To start the day with boisterous rivalry
To each his choice, right, wrong, or wise.

As usual, a very busy day had begun
For friends Jimmy, Gregg and John.
Mealtimes were no end of teasing;
Master Jimmy was bold and pleasing.

Bright Jimmy, a really sporting fellow,
Spirited, fair, was fun to follow;
Frank, fearless, the very best friend,
Handsome Jimmy was always mischief bent.

And so it went from day to day
Until the Lord decreed destiny's way,
Lightning fatally struck at Jimmy.
Lamenting his loss, we cherish his memory.

TODAY'S FLOWERS

A vase of flowers
A drop of dew—
Violets picked
All too few.

A drop of rain
A wave of a hand—
The corn that grows
Across our land.

Belief in God
Like a touch on the head,
Nice warm house
Comfortable bed.

The fresh air blowing
Kinship and talk—
Thinking of thoughts
A good long walk.

Hoping for better things
Glad they're not worse—
Memories grown dear
Pennies in a purse.

Working and happy
The hours fly by—
Truthful always
And not a lie.

Seeing the sky
Knowing God is there;
Living without worries
Always caring

Today's flowers open—
Beautiful and sharing.

JESUS WALKED AMONG THEM (A Song)

(Lyrics written by author; music by George Liberace Studio of Hollywood, Calif. Released toward end of 1971 by M.S.R. Records of Hollywood, Calif.)

First verse: Jesus is my Savior and of all who go astray;
Jesus walks with me, today and ev'ry day.
If you're in need of help, He's there to
show the way;
All you need to do is believe on Him and pray.
Jesus walked among them, all the weary men;
Jesus talked to all of them and bound their
hearts to Him.

Second verse: Jesus walks among us still, as He always
will,
If we but reach up and try to fulfill
His plan for our lives; we'll soon get back
On the right track, hooked to His pow'r,
Source of strength n' direction in ev'ry
hour.
We, appliances of God, must hook onto
His pow'r.

Chorus: When I am weak God makes me strong;
Where there's injustice God rights the wrong.
His light of truth banishes the dark;
For fire of enthusiasm, He lights the spark.
I'll walk with Him who lights the way;
Do what He'd have me do each day.
I'll stay with Him who makes me strong;
Sing to Him who gives me song.

JOY OF CREATION

To feel the zest of doing, to sing,
To drop an idea on the wing,
To bake a cake that's better eating,
To make a dress that's flattering,
To paint a picture, write a song—
Then you feel that you belong!

JOURNEY UNKNOWN

I die because I care to live no more;
My dreams have all turned into nothingness.
The aspirations I once loved so much
Are like the dregs within a glass of wine.

Gone is all flavor and the zest for life—
Gone are all the small cares of the day.

The stars come out;
The cloak of night enfolds me
As I start on my lonely way.

* * *

RENDEZVOUS WITH DESTINY

Waves mount to a shocking crescendo
        Where angry seas are running high;
Where dangerous tensions have to break
        Beneath a dark and threatening sky.

There is the magic of broad horizons
        Far beyond the churning sea;
There is light, faith, and hope
        In my rendezvous with destiny.

382

THE MORNING OF DESTRUCTION

I woke up one morning; it was too quiet and calm.
Could this have been the aftermath of the dropping
of the bomb?
There came no chirping from the birds
And from the radio there came no words.
Through my body ran a strange sensation,
I went outside to cure my temptation,
But to my surprise this was no imagination:
This whole damn world was in a state of ruination.
I stood there for hours feeling so strange,
Those buildings I once knew were now rearranged.
The cold war had come and the cold war had passed,
And the morning of destruction was here at last.
I couldn't feel love, I couldn't feel pity;
But I knew one thing—there was no more city.
As I walked through the streets of trash and rubble,
In the faraway distance a mushroom-shaped bubble—
The final end to all that past trouble.
And just yesterday the grass was so green,
And the people and places and all was serene,
And my younger brother would have turned sixteen.
And yesterday as I was up there flying,
The Big Three, the U.N.—one was lying,
Contemplating for today how the people would be dying.
And now the radiation is coming toward me
And I'll just wait and I won't resist,
For when you know you'll never be kissed,
What good is it for you to exist?
And just last night I heard a song called
"Eve of Destruction."
Could this have been a coincidence?
Or a reasonable deduction?

RUN, SON, RUN!

Run, Son, Run!
The devil is after my son.
He's got death in his hands
And a lie on his tongue.
Run, Son, Run!

Run, Son, Run!
Your beautiful life has just begun.
He's out here looking another to claim,
To strip of respect and make cringe in shame.
Run, Son, Run!

Run, Son, Run!
Recognize him when he comes.
He's dressed in beauty and exudes false light;
He whispers, "Sleep all day, and prowl all night."
Run, Son, Run!

Run, Son, Run!
You've accepted the Word,
Which is power from on high.
Run to the Christ, who promised in Him you'd
        never die.
Run, Son, Run!

PLEASURE IN THE AFTERNOON

Jamil
Vision. . .illusion?
No, real.
Loveliness slinking under the sheet behind
            the obscuring drapes;
Smoldering, lubricous, opening like the peelings
            coming off lush grapes;
Just feel.

* * *

A MIGHTY CIVILIZATION?

Lo, the curling Titian waves
Unfurling wantonly across an unconscionable sea,
Forever hurling the master craft
Where prescribes the man in purple!

* * *

DEPRESSION

Truth is
An impediment, an abomination to politicians,
Except where it can be woven into flags of deceit,
To corral the people into situations of confusion.
But I collect data and draw from it the lines of
            consequences
And consequently I know where all deceits lead.
I talk and talk but no one listens,
Because people like the familiar confusion
Their politicians have conditioned them to;
Nevertheless, truth is—
And one midnight it is going to knock on the door.

Olinda D. Tavares

WAITING

At the Grocers
I wait in line
    Patiently—
bidding my time!

At the restaurant
    I wait
For the food,
    on my plate!

The beauty parlor
    let's forget—
I WAIT until
I break out in a sweat!

    Half an hour I sat
At the laundromat,
Waiting for my clothes
to be cleaned by that
big machine!

    You work every day
But must WAIT till
    Friday for your pay!

If you're ill and go to
    the doctor
You WAIT, until
"Drop dead" is what
    you ought'er!

You fall in love and
What do you do?
You WAIT, 'til the day
He says "I LOVE YOU!"

A ring on the finger
was WAITED for—
Down the aisle he would
                    bring her—
His wife—forevermore!

She WAITS for him
to come home from work,
Only to find she forgot
the coffee to perk!

        To be a parent
        You must WAIT;
nine months spent
from the day of fate!

We WAIT for our children
            to grow up—
for the day that our
            children
Will fill our cup—

With coffee and Coffeemate
            we WAIT to drink. . .
It's too hot, so we WAIT—
Or throw it down the sink!

No matter where you go—
No matter what you do—
to (WAIT) is the Mighty Moe
for me, and for you!

And so we WAIT and WAIT—
Until we are old and gray,
In the end we WAIT
for the BURIAL DAY!

YOU PASS ME BY

A soul with no poison
   Is often lost,
His friends unchosen,
Reputation its cost—

Stripped of his dignity
he goes along his way,
dreaming of affinity,
someone with him to stay—

This soul is lonely
And he is sad!
For YOU he needs—only
YOU cannot be had!

It takes courage
To live in this world!
There is no refuge
From the vicious whirl.

Oh, hand me your hand
And look into my eye,
My heart crumbled like sand
As you passed me by!

Stop for a moment!
Think what you've done!
Tho my back is bent,
I'm still your son!

I would but cry,
If tears would come—
As you pass me by
And SPIT! like some!

Oh, God help me!
Take me away—
This I cannot see,
And I don't want to stay!

(Written for a poor soul—
a man who was considered a
genius—who played any instrument
that was handed him since he was
five years old without ever having
studied music; orphaned at 14;
his life ruined by drink.)

PEACE

The Healing of Peace is priceless—
It is the purity of wisdom and Love,
The Healing of Peace is priceless
For it is from the Octave above;
The Healing of Peace is priceless,
Great Cosmic Law, make mankind see—
Peace is the Healing power of the
        "Christ of Galilee,"
And it can Heal the wounds of hate
        for Eternity;
The Healing of Peace is priceless
And so is Your Love to ALL Life—
        and to me.

* * *

MIRACLES OF LOVE

Thou art the Tonal notes in Life's Symphony,
    A melodious undertone of love, peace and beauty;

Thou art the simplicity of Cosmic power,
    Breathing of growth, forgiveness and rest,
The swing of Life Divinely blest;
    Thou art the heartbeat of humanity,
The Eternal Flame of Life, Light's pulsing power—
    God's perfect harmony;
Thou art the God Presence's creative power,

A heavenly blending of Universal sound;
    Thou art a rose,
A star, lovely, divine—
    Men's souls you entwine;
Through Life's Symphony your Tonal notes blend
    And sing
Of God's Love, softly, exquisitely as an angel's wing.

390

THE BIG QUESTION

PROCLAIM: PROCLAIM: our wondrous fame,

A reason for a bell—a reason for its name:

"THE LIBERTY BELL."

Religious freedom for those intelligent;
A Supreme Being, His power to relent;

This symbol of Freedom—This Majestic Monument

"THE LIBERTY BELL."

"PROCLAIM LIBERTY THROUGHOUT ALL THE LAND
UNTO ALL THE INHABITANTS THEREOF." (LEVITICUS
XXV.10.)

In large round letters inscribed, but cracked by the

First stroke for a test of its sound. Leaving a question

And hearts to yearn; the answer yet to learn:

>Did it crack because it could not peal
>Half-truths of freedom and victories revealed?

>Did it muffle its sound, become brittle with fear,
>Protesting "Make me over—I cannot hang here?"

Politicians were puzzled and intensified through long hours

  Of pondering; they had to decide:

The story of our Nation must be told;
Break up the Bell—add new to the old;
Liquify its elements—recast—remold—
(Maybe the Bell should be solid gold.)

Two workmen labored hard and long;
In 1753 a new Liberty Bell was hung.

Two thousand eighty pounds in resonant tone
Chimed o'er the land in celebration.

Twelve feet of circumference, lip-bound
Resounding heroic deeds renowned.

Seven feet six inches around the crown
Crying "EVERYWHERE! EVERYWHERE! Let freedom be foun

From the crown to the lip measures three feet in length
Foretelling the foundation of America's strength.

The three-foot two-inch clapper of the Liberty Bell
Has many, many stories to tell:

> Beginning with the defiance of the Mother Country's rule,
> When it rang out the battle cry and victory news—

> Peace with our Mother Country—A New Nation is born;
> Peal out for Independence and a Declaration.

Then it solemnly tolled for funerals of: George Washington,
Jefferson, Adams (A Nation in tears); and other Great Men
Who led this country through its beginning years.
But, it cracked
Again in 1835 (while tolling the death of the United States
Supreme Court Chief Justice, James Marshall).

YES, ANOTHER SPLIT DOWN ITS GREAT METAL SIDE,
Again the pondering, this time to decide—
RETIRE THE LIBERTY BELL; its crack is too wide.

One hundred and thirty-eight years later, in 1973,
The Bell in humble silence has a message for you and me.

Unknown decisions affecting your children and mine,
Grands, Great-grands, Generations up the line,
In truth—their minds and souls to refine.

This National Majestic Monument

Of a Christian Nation Heaven-sent,

Under God's watchful Eye, our Flag unfurled,

Shaped in His favor for a Peaceful World.

WHO LIVES TO 142?

If you should reach the good old age of
　One hundred and forty-two,
Just think of all the lovely things
　About to come to you.

But now you're in a leaking boat—
　The name? "Devaluation"—
And you may wait a hundred years
　For "long-run" estimation.

Well, what we need is "short-run" help
　To pay the plumber's bill,
Or meet the doctor's heavy charge
　In case someone is ill.

I do not think the longer life
　Means much to me or you,
With food so high we'll never reach
　One hundred forty-two.

A CHANGE OF FACE

It's always been a pleasure,
　　When looking at TV,
To recognize the faces
　　That are like old friends to me.

But now that men have fallen
　　For beard, and mustache too,
It's hard to recognize my friends
　　The way I used to do.

For often in some places
　　The hair is still quite thin,
But oftener the hair has grown
　　Where hair has never been.

We have a "day" for everything,
　　So let's add to the book
A "day" when men can demonstrate
　　The way they used to look.

(Published in *Manhattan East* February 20, 1973)

Beatrice Todd

TO MY LANDLORD

I picked up peelings from the floor,
I looked above and there were more.
An ugly leak is what I saw:
             My Landlord.

I phoned the super in my place.
He took some time to show his face.
We disagreed about the case:
             My Landlord.

It seemed to me my super lied;
He said the cause was rain outside.
"It's faulty plumbing," I replied:
             My Landlord.

(Published in *Manhattan East* January 23, 1973)

1973

I'm wishing such a lot of things
 For Nineteen Seventy-Three—
They number more than hairs on head
 And all the ships at sea.

I wish for equal justice
 And an end to all the crime
To last forever in this world,
 Not only "in our time."

But most of all I wish and pray
 This senseless War may cease,
And we may know the priceless joy
 Of Universal Peace.

(Published in *Manhattan East* January 2, 1973)

LOSS

I am so lone and sad,
Though I had times quite glad.
Still, no one could cheer me up
Or clean the bitter cup
When I lost the best friend I ever had.

I had been warned before:
"Leave it to the mediator."
But impatience soon won out,
And I am left with doubt
If any chances remain in store,

Till a soft hand touched my back
And restored the courage that I lack.
A quiet smile, a kind thought;
No longer fear I the foe fought,
Now that I have acquired the knack.

So tired, yet must make the most
Of my rest, a strengthening dose,
And back to the daily grind;
Excercise my hands and mind.
Still knowing that SOURCE is ever close.

ANSWER

It takes a lifetime to grow,
To learn, to understand.
And when our time comes to go
All dissolves in the sand.

But this can't be the answer
To the meaning of man.
There is a higher Power—
It goes beyond our span.

Take what life gives and add some;
There is meaning to all.
Though cognizance may not come,
We must answer the call.

No, it all can't be for nought—
Our striving and searching,
And all life's living has taught—
There has to be meaning.

Else why the accomplishment,
The progress of mankind,
If not for his betterment?
This in itself is a find!

Bits of goodness leave their mark,
Effects go on and on.
Comers find it not as dark
When life they come upon.

Our sojourn 'tis not in vain,
Our precious gifts we leave.
With each passing comes some gain—
This we know we achieve!

MEMORIAL ACROSTIC

TO

PRESIDENT JOHN FITZGERALD KENNEDY

J-oin the world in humble tribute
O-n these days of grave concern,
H-ush the hate, the greed, the envy,
N-ever falter, be like men.

F-ailure spells disease and death
I-n all that noble men should be.
T-hus he strived to work for freedom,
Z-est in work will make men free;
G-o the limit, spare not the "nth" degree,
E-re the world may see the light,
R-egard the glory of its might
A-s the truth comes marching on.
L-ove will conquer, hate be gone!
D-one will be the job that's right.

K-nights have fought battles of yore,
E-nriched the world with deeds of fame,
N-ever enticed by loot or lust,
N-ever betrayed their knightly name;
E-nduring great hardships to win the throng,
D-ying like martyrs without refrain; in
Y-onder field, to right what's wrong.

TRIBUTE TO MY MOTHER
(MOTHER'S KISS AND MOTHER'S LOVE)

Happy are those who have felt
Their tender faces caressed
By a sweet, maternal kiss!
Happy are those who have heard
The maternal lullaby,
Who were tenderly rocked to sleep
By a sweet voice from the sky.

She watches you as you grow
With her tender, loving care;
She will guide as you would fawn
For her love is sweet and true;
Her understanding will glare
As the light which glares at dawn.

As you grow and come to think
And your heart is lit with love,
Render homage to your mother,
For she is the one and only one
Who will cater without bother
To the needs of son and daughter.

Bow your head and kiss the dust
That she walks on, and the cradle
Which rocked you to peaceful slumber.
Touch ye and without grumble
List and carry her commands,
For a mother's love forever stands.

When her hair has turned to silver
And her step's no longer strong,
Lock your arms around her bosom,
Guide her through life's painful throng;
For life's trials and deep sorrows
Are soon forgot with a mother's love.

TO JUAN PINOY de LA CRUZ

To denounce poverty, graft and corruption
Is to cramp your old tradition.
Get your shovel, rake, and hammer,
Build your country into a new nation.

Demonstration is not the answer,
Nor revolution that is bloody;
But teach your children humility—
Love thy neighbors as thyself.
Earthquakes and other calamities are signs
It's time to get up and work hard.
Explore your land down into the ocean;
Have no fear except to our Almighty.

XODUS '70

Dream while you're still young,
Dream while the sky is bright;
Dream when the river is up high,
Dream. . .Dream. . .Dream.

Write all your plans right now,
Write all your bright ideas;
Write while you are inspired,
Write. . .Write. . .Write.

Build for your future now,
Build for your children's tomorrow;
Build while you're still strong—
Build. . .Build. . .Build.

Go where your future is,
Go where happiness will be;
Go when opportunity is ready—
Go. . .Go to the U.S.A.

WHO CARES?

Once I was young and fair of face;
I loved the entire human race.
      Who cares?
I studied hard all during school,
Tried to live by the golden rule.
      Who cares?
When I grew up and went to work
Responsibilities I didn't shirk—
      Who cares?
I kept the faith thru storm and strife;
Worked hard, paid taxes all my life.
      Who cares?
A president I cannot be
Can't even sail across the sea.
      Who cares?
I'll ne'er attend the revellers' ball,
I have no social life at all.
      Who cares?
I'm not important to the world,
I'm just a lonely working girl.
      Who cares?
My country's treasures I won't see,
A White House guest I'll never be,
      Who cares?
I'm aging now. . .Life's song is sung;
The old must make way for the young.
      Who cares?
Soon, rest in peace beneath the sod;
When that time comes, except for God,
      Who cares?

Carol Ellen Warden

YOUTH GONE BY

Will you recall the days of our youth,
When life was ours and ours alone?
Oh, to have known then that life was an instant,
And that that instant soon would be gone.

The pony rings and children's dreams
And autumn leaves and woodland streams
Are owned by other children now,
And fill the wonder of a child's sweet vow.

Reach out to touch the days gone by—
Reach out to touch and wonder why
Children can't know of Life's cold stream;
Adults can't leave the world by dreams.

Imprisoned by Time, we live our brief lives
And pass away unremembered.
For all the great things a man lives and strives,
They join him in dust soon after he dies.

(ELLEN) BLUE GIRL

"The camera takes the soul away,"
I heard an Indian say.
Your picture shows
Just where it goes;
The negatives proclaim
Memorials to same.
The prints attest
The soul divest.

The moon takes heaven's light away,
Yet lets it in the darkness play.
Within my room your picture lies
As distant lights within the skies
Hasten toward earth, a hopeless goal,
To tint its clays and prove its soul.

Blue Girl, the incense burned the vase
You Semite of Grace.
Send runners to every tribe,
Dream pools, sweat baths, smoke, talk, bribe.
Amanuensis (Polaroid);
Barometer, both full and void.
We're dewdrops on the mountain
But seconds pois'd—then join the fountain.

George R. Wesley
Bee Sweatt

DEWDROP

One tiny diamond dewdrop
Trapped an orgy of sunlight
In its heart, and turned
A sparkling mirror to nothingness.

* * *

THE WRITER

Give me Eden or give me Hell—
I'll write on fig leaves or brimstone.

* * *

DREAMER

In psychedelic color clutch the dream!
Fathom the depths of the nether side of the
          soul,
Never completed, but like the wandering
          stream
Sluice through the metamorphic cavern old.
Mine the deadly pain of failing view
While fool's gold tingles the nerves of
          hope.
Watch the dream loom bright and near you
Then fade to psychedelic wisps of smoke.
Hear the loud wind roar through hell,
As colors blur and the dream transcends
          your page,
And taste the galling, bitter, vapor shell
Of rage replacing empty rage.
The stench of the flailing self will soon
          grow less,
And a taste of life restores the lost
          caress.

CHRISTMAS EVE PRAYER

Christmas Eve—and each gift, wrapped with tender love
And thoughtfully chosen colored paper and ribbon,
Has been carefully placed and replaced beneath the tree
Resplendent with countless sparkling ornaments.

Late afternoon shadows are creeping over our world—
The sun drops silently from sight, its rays
Reaching up like loving hands, warm and golden,
For a final caress of the satiny sky.

Night tucks downy opaqueness around each home.
Here and there a searching eye of light peeps through
The folds of the deepening darkness of evening,
And shines like a jewel resting upon rich velvet.

Softly the strains of "Silent Night, Holy Night"
Interweave the wintry air—ever so gently—
With a melody of reverence and beauty—and
Our hearts catch and hold the sweet refrain.

The last tender notes lingeringly fade into the night. . .
Swells then, and echoes far, this ageless carol:
"Joy to the World, The Lord is Come!"—and
We lift our thoughts and eyes toward the heavens.

Hope, precious hope, the needed sustenance of life,
Reflects a rekindling; a responsive glow within
Permeates our very souls, and earnestly we pray
For peace on earth, good will toward men—all men!

NOSTALGIA

If I could be a child again
        And wander free in field and glen,
To follow streams that wound or rushed
        Or murmured peacefully or gushed,
I'd think it was a perfect day
        If I should find upon my way
A green and grassy fairy ring
        Or hear an unseen wild bird sing;
To see a trout leap up and then
        Hide quiet from the fisherman;
To find some periwinkle shells,
        Hear faintly tinkling cattle bells.

I'd think it was a perfect day
        If I returned home tired from play
With grimy hands and wind-blown hair
        And found my mother waiting there.
She'd say, "Now run and wash your face
        And at the table take your place.
With all this wandering everywhere
        You must be hungry as a bear!"
She'd help me brush the tangles out
        While hearing me tell all about
Discoveries in sun and shade
        Upon this journey I had made.

Then, clean and warm and fully fed
        I'd climb the stairs and find my bed,
And drowsiness at last would win
        When, after prayers, she tucked me in.
If I could pass once more that way—
        Oh, that would be a perfect day.

Alfreda Williamson

THE STORM

Silently we stood there,
Waiting for its approach.
It rumbled into our lives,
Into the unsettlement of folly.

The rain warned of its following;
It, too danced into ourselves.
We let it—it was welcomed.
It settled leafy matters,
It gave the day a beauty it needed.
So we receded into privacy.

A world of thoughts and illusions. . .
Perhaps a little time of love and peace.

The wind whispered by us
Under the door,
On its way to give greetings
To the hail
That shot the windows
Like sand flung against unbreaking unity.

Then, too, it all receded,
Leaving only the soft murmurs
Of the rain, the distant thunder,
And something steady. . .
Existence.

TO FINALLY REACH THE END

As I look into my soul in search of peace of mind,
And find no answer clear enough to ease the pains within;
As life grows old and days cold and memory unkind,
My heart pulsates its deepest throb to finally reach the end.

Disillusioned thoughts throughout the day, optimistic all
in all,
Have made my life a sacrifice of respect and inner pride,
Until what's left is an ugly brain my soul humbly appalls,
And restless nights and horrid dreams, wishing long ago I'd
died.

Sometimes I think it's been too long without love to see
me through,
But I can't recall the smell it had or the color of its
leaves;
The memory of her is not as fresh as when it was really true,
I've forgotten love, I tell myself, and make myself believe.

Insanity creeps into my mind, rusting hinges on the door;
Paranoia erupts and overflows in stinging agony.
I've forsaken the endless search for truth; vision growing
poor;
A loser I must be; in fact, there is no truth for me.

Alone, I am a helpless man without want or need,
And deep inside I realize that death is my only friend.
It seems my life's an empty book open for all to read,
My life, I pray, like all tasteless things, to reach the end.

A GRAVE MISTAKE

Footsteps paced to and fro
Upon the earth above his head,
Shuffling toward no and all directions
As he lay helplessly amongst the dead.
And nothing could I do
To unearth the grave that he had made,
Imprisoning a poor, foolish soul
Kept breathing in its grave.
Fires from hell encasted the tomb
So all who dared would know,
That worshiping but the One True God
Led not to heaven nor hell below.

MOMUS AND THE SHADOW OF DEATH

Her lips she pressed against the slab;
  the marble, cold and gray as ash
No place could find within her heart,
  or counsel give or comfort cheer—
For it was death's own bier. The
  heart within her, cold and lone,
Went forth to beg a crumb of stone
  from out that earthen lethal strand—
Any place a spirit ran. Material ease
  had been her lot, and there no place
She built against that day when justice
  fell and cast her away. The hard
Cut glitter of the cold, jewels glistening in red gold, and knowing not the
Pinch of want, had taught her heart to
  seek the pleasant things which
Teach the heart to taunt. Had she but
  known the torture, grief, and shame
Of one just soul unjustly slain—
  had she but fought the bitter fight
Of those betrodden souls around, she
  might have learned of God's great
Might, and not have made her bier the
  ground. But she had followed Momus
To her doom; her heart lay heavy, dead
  within her tomb. The GUT of that
Strange woman who, not loving God, had
  placed her hope in MAMMON and made
Her bier the sod.

A COMETH

What power drove me to earth

In search for a rock I know not.

I saw it as a girl whose hair is that of gold

That spread'th for many light years long;

Whose every spark of life seem'th mine.

But mine is all but a short life;

I seek eternal love,

For I shall not be here for long.

* * *

OF TIME

Boundless is the love

That survives thru time,

Like the timeless waves

That never stop their rocking.

JET FLIGHT

It would sound silly after coming back to
earth again, but I have never seen so far.

The blue of the sky—deep—much deeper and
much clearer than from solid ground;
The cloud picture—changing continually—
thunderheads—billowing bubbles of cotton
clouds—stretching as far as the eye could see
in all directions.

Thin slivers of clouds—tipped at crazy angles
—flashes of sunlight on pure white cotton—
reach out and touch the infinite.
The colors, the purity, the dimensions. . .

Man is a mere speck. Jump off the wing tip
and tumble like a tiny pebble through endless
puffs of clouds—somersaulting earthward—
vanishing from sight.

* * *

PINTAIL

Three pintails, losing altitude
against the setting sun,
tore in at high speed
in very tight formation,
and settled at last
on the water
for the
night.

STILL WONDERING

When I was a little girl, busy at play,
I wondered what it would be like to be married someday;
To watch our children busy at play,
And send them to school to learn each day.

I married a man from far, far away;
We watched our little children busy at play.
We sent them to school to learn every day,
And after graduation each went his own way.

Now we are grandparents, we are happy and gay.
We watch our grandchildren busy at play;
The time will come when we'll be going away;
Where will we go? Who can say?

* * *

CHILD'S PERPLEXITY

Oh, Moon! You're tangled in that tree;
What can I do to set you free?
You are so high, the snow is so deep;
Mommy says, "Now you must go to sleep."

Next morn—
Oh my! dear Moon, where did you go?
Who set you free I do not know.
Were you tangled in that tree,
Or was the thinking wrong in me?

I LOVE SUNDAY MORNINGS

I love Sunday mornings,
    with the freedom they bring,
After a week of routine,
    And when the church bells ring
I join in worship—
    Not always in the usual way—
But whether I go to church or not,
    I love the day.

* * *

THERE IS CHARM IN WINTER NIGHTS

There is charm in winter nights,
    clear and still;
When the cold cuts and bites.
    I always thrill
To see the moon high overhead,
    so bright,
That where it's light is shed,
    the night
Is such a lovely winter's view.
    Old, ages ago,
Yet re-occurring, always new—
    Moon and snow.

SPRING

Spring: that will be when the snow is gone,
Leaving puddles of water on the back lawn.
Papers and litter in every nook;
Dirty, unkept—that's how it will look.

Then comes the day the first robin is seen,
And thru the brown stubble grass that is green.
As out-of-doors takes on eye appeal;
Jeepers! Spring! How wonderful you feel!

BABY GIRL

My fingers entwine each little curl
As I hold to my heart my baby girl.
To us she's the sweetest ever born
But always cutest in the early morn,
Climbing down from her little bed
With sleepy eyes and tousled head.
She toddles around all the day
Lisping and singing in her baby way.
Her golden curls and dear blue eyes
Are sunshine to us—for she seldom cries—
And as I drink in the beauty of her innocent face,
Its sweet expressions fill me with grace.
For I know she's a gift from heaven above
Reflecting God and His wonderful Love.

* * *

PRAYER OF THE UNBORN

Before I go to earth, Dear God,
I'll say a prayer to You:
Let me be good and wholesome
For the ones that wait for me.
Endow me not with beauty
If it will make me vain,
Or else I ask to not be born
And spare my mother pain.
But let me make my loved ones proud
And my mother and father happy, too;
In other words, Dear God,
Let me resemble you.

ODE TO CHILD VICKY

Double-coated white innocent,
With aura of saintly
Perfumed fragrancy. . .

Gossamer celestial,
Purity smiling through
Trusting perceptive eyes. . .

Nylon chiffon-like voice,
Exercising gentle flowing
Sounds resembling harmonious tunes. . .

* * *

TO A MAN OF COLORS

My thoughts have you formed as a man
For all moments of color:
Moments tinted with blueness;
Moments splashed of redness;
Times of whiteness
Tinged with purple;
Times of blackness
Tinged with brown;
Days of glowing
Red and green;
Days of sparkling
Blue and green.
An era of never-ending arching rainbows;
A man of spectrum;
An image formed prismatically;
A man for all
Moments and colors.

A TOAST TO J.F.K.

May your dreams, insights, and torches
Continue to light and illuminate
In all men's minds and hearts. . .

And may your dreams, insights, and torches
Survive as long as the wonders of Egypt
Survived in giving mankind
Magnificence!

Which we once had seen. . .

* * *

HATE NO MORE

Once you thought you discovered
Why A. Hitler asphyxiated Jewish persons.
Your proclaimation of discovery read:
"Discovered. . .A Hitler killed
Jewish persons because of
Extreme hatred for
The Son of God,
A royal Jew."

Since that time
Your discovery has been followed by
A creation of a peace chant:
"Forget the unforgivable. . .
Forgive the unforgettable. . .
Remember. . .
The Son of God
Will die no more!
Hate. . .no more.
Hate. . .no more.
Hate. . .no more."

WHAT IS IT THAT WE CAN CLAIM?

Even tho I may be dead
Don't cry on your bed .
With this life that goes so fast
Someday we'll meet again .
And cry on each other's shoulders again ,
Not with grief, but joy ,
Just like many other girls and boys
Who have long been separat'd .

When I die I'll go
To someplace I don't know much about ,
But I hope it's nice ,
'Cause this world will never suffice .
I wish I could see
A better world for you and I ,
But I'll settle for what I have
For if I do not. . .

Where else can I be ?
What else can I do? A few unanswerable questions
I bet you would agree
To let me go and see
If I could build that new life .
But who could we fool
A Utopia we could never tool .
Our life is what we have, what we make, what we put into it .

And if it's not up to par ,
Who have we to blame ?
What is it that we can claim
That cannot be made better ?
No one is under obligation to human society ,
Except ones who feel "It's my duty "
You ?
Me ?

422

John F. Wysokinski

EMOTIONS

Arms
Encircling
Bodies
A
Fervent
Kiss .
Looks
Into
Each other's
Eyes .
Emotions
Turn'd on .
Love .
Strong
Deep feeling, and
Great affection
Passionate
Ardent
Devotion
For
Each
Other .

AUTUMN BOUQUET

Summer long over, long over our love,
　　Phantom hands bring thee an autumn bouquet—
Pale, drooping poppies and faded foxglove;
　　Withered dead daisies to frost fallen prey;
Lilacs and violets well-watered by tears,
With putrid roots where the earthworm adheres;
　　Livid-white lilies besmeared by black mud;
Yesterday's asters grown brown with decay;
　　Roses dyed red by a suicide's blood,
Plucked from cold ground of the grave where I lay!

* * *

DEMOLISHED MANSIONS

Beneath the wrecking ball they fall,
　　These towered dowagers of stone,
And history dies in days; years razed
　　With once-proud walls laid prone:
Their passing few will rue—this new
　　World has no room to house the old,
And many a ghost aghast goes cast
　　Into the outer cold.

424

Josephine Zajkoski

THE DEVIL WITH YOU

The time of the Devil is at hand—
    the Pope fears for his faithful flock;
The time of the Devil rules the land
    for the faithful hear his knock.

The faithful of man accepts this myth,
    giving to the Devil his due,
With the form of the beast to fulfill the part,
    free to entice as the human would do.

The destiny of man has its furrowed course,
    like the tracks which lead to town.
Friendly faces will greet the former host
    when he is clad in the shining gown.

The Devil, they say, has had his sway
    to corrupt the young and the old;
To lead to perdition lives of pure intent,
    to return not one to the fold.

This grandeur of power has no equality
    in the realm of beast or man;
What being is found in the life of God
    to equal the Creator and His plan?

Free lives have the power to choose what they do,
    to follow the desires of the heart;
Fearsome friends lay false claims to the evil's deeds,
    relating to the Devil his part.

The force of life is both for evil and good,
    the extension of right is wrong;
Foolish the man who in the world exists,
    who finds life the freedom's song.

Whether he is called Satan or Life,
   his being must come from God.
This truth is the falsehood taught by all
   who admit to the devil his clod.

The pitchfork leaves in the mind of man
   the symbol of the Devil's power,
Forgetting the fact that the frugal life
   will turn it lovingly toward a flower.

Truth, to the man obsessed with sin,
   has no life, no fire to burn,
For the thoughts that have the message true
   find their place with the ash in the urn.

Strange is the stranger in the unknown land,
   stranger still his ideas perverse;
The mind trained toward ill thoughts and desires
   sets the gears of freedom in reverse.

The strength of the foe is within the self,
   the strength of goodwill, too;
To accord to the Devil all ill acts
   is to admit the Devil—is you.

AZNAVOUR

(Dedicated to the international star,
Charles Aznavour, one of the greatest
talents of our time.)

I rest within the loneliness of my life
  Upon the glass night of tortured dreams—
    when Aznavour comes through
              my stereo
  and smashes the harsh veneer
      of my scarlet-tinselled world.
He sings of love and fading youth;
    of "Venice Blue" and "Yesterday,"
  and at that moment
      I am but his servant—
        caught in a vicious rage of hell;
        menaced by the anguish
                  of unrealized
                  love.

* * *

THE FUTILE CLIMB

Twisted, snarled branches,
Shorn of all ornament,
They stretch upward
Like the Tower of Babel—
Never to reach God,
But to perish in their plight.

427

POET, WHY DO YOU DIE?

(Dedicated to Vasile Posteuca, former Professor
of Languages at Mankato State College in
Minnesota.)

Poet, why do you die when lesser men
live?

Poet, who gave so much of yourself to fight
error,

Thrust from your motherland for what you believed
right.

Why did you see wrong as real rather than
unreal?

Did you know that a successful error is but a
defeated truth?

Poet, why do you die when lesser men
live?

AUTHOR INDEX

AUTHOR INDEX—New Voices

431

433

TITLE INDEX

TITLE INDEX—New Voices

437

438

439

440

442

443

444

445

PHOTOGRAPHIC SECTION

The numbers in italics locate the page numbers of the author's work.

Wesley M. Alden *(2–3)*

M. Crawford Anderson *(4–5)*

Louise B. Armstrong *(10–14)*

Evelyn M. Artis *(15)*

Frieda Migge Bair *(17)*

Josephine Batis *(22)*

Eva Beaver *(24—25)*

Princess Orelia Benskina *(27—28)*

Constance Marie Benson   *(29—31)*

H. Lee Benson   *(32—33)*

Carmen Blumenkron   *(44—47)*

"Taken when she was 24 years old"

Roger Boisclair   *(49)*

Anne Sophia Bullard *(61–63)*

Clara L. Butler *(65)*

Elmer J. Carpenter *(75–76)*

Akintola Cole *(82-86)*

Felix Cotten   *(103–104)*

Peter Curto   *(109–111)*

Ruth I. Davis   *(114–115)*

Helen Del Valle   *(118–121)*

Rev. Clydrow Durbney   *(129—130)*

Mary K. Ebbert   *(132—133)*

Margaret B. Foertsch   *(158—159)*

Margaret Patricia Fox   *(160)*

Dorothy V. Gittins   *(175—177)*

Alleyne Gower   *(180)*

Johnnie Hobson Griffin   *(183)*

Olga Hahn   *(185—187)*

Josephine Hallquist   *(188—191)*

Diana Hayward   *(199)*

Emeline Henderson   *(201—203)*

Louise Butts Hendrix   *(206—208)*

Margaret Brady Jackson *(222—223)*   Elaine Hoisington Johnson *(225—227)*

Gertrude C. Knight *(241—242)*   Harriet Trehus Kvingedal *(245—250)*

Jean Layer *(256)*

Irene Vannelli Lindgren *(260)*

H. S. McFarland *(269—272)*

Ruth Moorefield *(289)*

Charles R. Morrison *(293)*

Leon Arnold Muller *(297)*

Michael J. Murphy *(298–299)*

Adele Murray *(300–301)*

C. W. Nelson *(304—306)*

Herbert W. Peters *(312—315)*

Rhoda B. Pierce *(316—320)*

William Prunty *(323—324)*

Opal Putman   *(326)*

Bertha Rives Quarles   *(327)*

John Robb   *(336)*

Donald E. Schwalke   *(351—352)*

Lloyd Donald Seager *(356)*   Violet Idell Settle *(358—361)*

Ruth R. Shepherd *(362—363)*

Reinold Shubert *(366—367)*   Olinda D. Tavares *(386—389)*

Robert L. Vialpando, Ph.D.   *(400–401)*   John Winthrop   *(415)*

P E A C E

In   Loving   Memory
James Woods
Mrs. Billie Backer (16)

Onie Mae Wright   *(419)*   Helen G. Wuerth   *(420–421)*